It's Not The Destination, But The Journey

Randy Durich

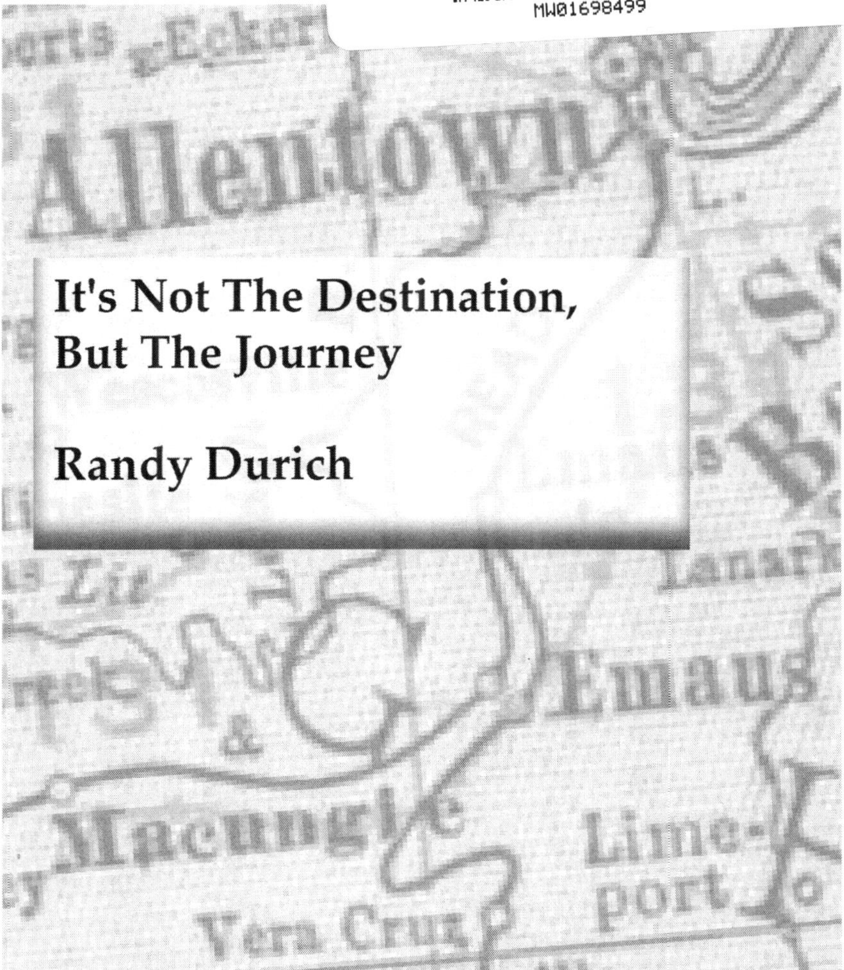

trimarkpress

Published by TriMark Press, Inc., Deerfield Beach, Florida.

Library of Congress Cataloging-in-Publication Data

It's Not The Destination, But The journey
By Randy Durich

p. cm.

ISBN: 978-1-943401-81-9
Library of Congress Control Number: 2020920153
J-20
10 9 8 7 6 5 4 3 2 1
First Edition
Printed and Bound in the United States of America

trimarkpress

A publication of TriMark Press, Inc.
368 South Military Trail
Deerfield Beach, FL 33442
800.889.0693

www.TriMarkPress.com

Dedication

Is it possible for one man to instill simultaneous fear and love in my heart? Did I quiver at the sound of the words, "Wait until your father gets home!" and at the same time, feel warmth whenever Dad spoke the words, "You did a nice job with that project, and I'm proud of you"? You bet I did.

Was I forever grateful for a mom who believed in me more than I believed in myself? You bet I was.

Together, they served up a banquet of memories.

This book is for them.

Acknowledgements

A special thank you to my daughter, Amy, an extremely talented graphic artist who created the artwork for the cover of this book.

In addition, I would like to thank my dear, sweet Nori for her tireless help with the editing of this book. Together, we shared thoughts and ideas to improve each of the pages in the original manuscript. I did my best, but her "second set of eyes" proved invaluable in telling the story.

Table of Contents

1.

The Beginning

I awoke to a bone-chilling cold, aware that I was dressed in the suit that my father bought for my high school graduation over a year earlier.

As sleep began to clear from my eyes, I surveyed my surroundings. Austere cinder block walls surrounded me, their pale white providing contrast to the slate gray tile floor. It occurred to me that I was lying on my overcoat, and the realization that not only was there no bed in this room, but no other furniture.

I was in Logan, Utah, 2,106 miles from Allentown, Pennsylvania – my home for the first nineteen years of my life. My world, my only world, and now this.

What brought me to this unusually cold September morning began with a conversation I had with a dear friend at a diner many months earlier.

But my story goes back farther, to a house in a six by six block section on the north side of Allentown, Pa. Although many wonderful people of Syrian and German descent made their home here, the neighborhood was mostly populated by Italian Americans and home to my father's Italian bakery, the Allentown Italian Club, as well as Russoli's and Stravino's Italian markets.

Row houses made up many of the neighborhoods in Allentown. Seven or eight homes were joined together and separated from another row of houses by a small alley. During warm summer evenings, our parents relaxed on their porch furniture taking in whatever breeze wafted through the streets. One could sit on his or her porch and look down the row over the short walls separating each house and see clear to the end of the row. A unique camaraderie existed between our neighbors. Everyone got along, and apart from an occasional disagreement, the people in our row were like family.

As our parents exchanged stories about the events of the day and read their evening newspapers, we played games on the sidewalks and streets in full view of them. It was an innocent time when front doors remained unlocked, and we played outside after dark, our parents knowing their children were safe.

Our neighborhood was an interesting blend of homes and industrial structures. Behind our row was the Bonney Forge - a factory that forged tools from white hot steel using enormous hammers that rattled our windows during the day and shook our beds at night when the third shift took over.

Across the street was the Hygrade silk mill whose massive looms wove thread into fabric while competing with the Bonney Forge for decibel domination! Behind the Hygrade was a trucking company teeming with tractor trailers arriving and departing all hours of the day and night.

Behind every house was a fenced- in yard containing a patch of lawn lovingly maintained by our parents, a task eventually passed onto their children. During laundry day, one could see bed sheets, pillow cases and clothing fluttering in the breeze. Most of us had electric dryers, but there was something special about slipping into bed between sheets that had been dried by the warm, summer air. It was especially satisfying to me because the sheets on my bed had been fashioned by my mother and my Nonna from the cloth flour sacks recycled from my father's bakery. They sewed the bags together to form bedsheets of a rather abrasive texture, and any help from the summer air and sun to soften them was welcomed.

Every yard had one special wash line known as the pulley line.

This line was joined by two pulley wheels – one near a window and the other attached to a pole at the end of the yard. One only had to attach an article of clothing on the line and "wheel" it to the yard. Dozens of plastic Holsum and Freihofer bread bags could be seen hanging on the pulley lines throughout the neighborhood. Mom would wash the empty bread bags and hang them on the pulley line to dry. Today, one only needs to pick up a box of Ziploc bags at the supermarket, but our moms were ahead of their time

During World War II, families on the home front planted gardens near their homes as a contribution to the war effort. These gardens were known as "Victory Gardens." Following the war's end, many of these gardens remained and became part of the American landscape. A parcel of land that sat between our homes and the Bonney Forge contained small victory gardens worked by every family in the neighborhood. The garden was a patchwork of cornstalks, lettuce and tomato plants and other vegetables tended to by our parents as well as their children during the spring and summer.

The summer months were a time for action! None of us wanted to waste a moment in the house having lunch. We chose, instead, to head to Russoli's market where we pooled our money and bought an eight pack of Morton's miniature salt shakers. These little containers of salt fit perfectly into our pockets and provided the proper seasoning for the various veggies available to us in our neighbors' gardens. It was the perfect deli for us. We simply called a timeout between innings, strolled across the street, and helped ourselves to an ear of corn, a tomato or whatever veggie tickled our fancy, and with a few shakes from our mini Morton container, had lunch! Washing the vegetable was never an option. A few swipes on our shirt, and it was good to go. Since most of the gardens were supplied with a hose, a quick guzzle of water and we were back to our ball game.

A gravel covered alley ran the length of the row houses between our yards and the Victory gardens. That alley was our Disneyland. Using our moms' brooms, we swept gravel to the side to create our marble courts. Each court contained three evenly spaced holes approximately five inches in diameter and three inches deep. The courts were the sites of some very serious marble competition. "Serious" because if one's marble was eliminated by a "killer" marble, that marble went permanently in another's marble bag.

Every so often, the bowling pins were replaced at the Italian Club, and the club officers gave us a set of old pins. After sweeping an entire "lane" of gravel, we used a spare pin as a bowling ball and slid it down the alley. Our designated pin boy removed the downed pins and returned the "ball" for a chance at the spare. One of the more devastating moments in our young lives came when the city replaced the gravel with a permanent layer of asphalt!

Losing our beloved alley to the asphalt truck, we moved on to new adventures. The Italian ladies did most of their shopping at the Great Atlantic and Pacific supermarket. The store's logo shone brightly in large, red letters - A&P - on a yellow background. Since most of our moms didn't drive, they walked to the market, bought and loaded their groceries in one of the A&P shopping carts, and promptly wheeled it home. There were so many carts scattered about our neighborhood, we used to refer to them as Allentown's mascots. One of the more industrious members of our gang discovered that the back end of one of these carts, when pried loose, could serve as an excellent cooking grate. We took the grate to a vacant lot behind the trucking company where we spent the better part of the day. Young boys and vacant lots just seem to go together. We built a perfect campfire ring from the rocks in the lot, set our new "grate" over the top, and we were ready for our next adventure.

Aerosol cans were uncommon at that time, but there was one exception – Rediwhip! We rummaged through everyone's trash cans and came up with a plethora of empty whipped cream cans. Building a nice, hot fire in our campfire ring, we set empty cans of Rediwhip on our A&P grate and ran for cover! Eventually, the can ignited and launched into the air like an Atlas Five rocket!

The back end of the vacant lot dropped off about fifteen feet to a set of railroad tracks. A large sour apple tree stood at the top of the embankment, overlooking the train tracks. We tied a rope onto one of the stronger limbs of the tree and waited for the train. Trains moving through the neighborhood traveled slowly. The sport was simple. We waited for a boxcar to pass by with its doors open. Timing was critical. Holding onto the rope, we jumped from the embankment, swung toward the moving train, and, hopefully, swung into the open box car and back out before becoming snagged on the open door. If our timing was slightly off, we simply crashed into the side of the boxcar.

When we returned home for supper, our parents had no idea that we had spent the afternoon blowing up whipped cream cans and launching ourselves at moving trains. Perhaps it was better that way.

2.

Always Baseball

Growing up in our neighborhood during the summer meant swimming at the Jordan Park, flashlight tag, hanging out at Doc's in the evening, and baseball. Every kid had his own glove, autographed by a Major League ballplayer, sure to make us better players. How could we miss if we were fielding ground balls with the same glove used by Alvin Dark or Tony Kubek or tracking down balls in the outfield with a Mickey Mantle or Ritchie Ashburn model? Those gloves were our pride and joy. We kept a baseball wrapped in the glove when we weren't using it to maintain the perfect pocket and rubbed them down with leather oil to keep them flexible.

We all had our own bat, usually purchased at Sweeny and Stalziz sporting goods store, a little shop in the basement of Frankie and Johnnie Stalziz's house. Again, the bats were signed by our favorite Major Leaguers and were certain to bring us unbridled success at the plate! Inevitably, our bat would sustain a crack, but, unlike the big-league guys who merely tossed them away and selected another one from their personal supply, we had to repair our bat. A few nails hammered into strategic locations in the damaged bat, followed by a healthy wrap of Dad's electrical tape, and our bat was good to go for another month or two. We could never understand why our fathers became so upset when they needed to repair a lamp only to find their supply of electrical tape was gone!

Occasionally, we ventured down to the Jordan park to play on one of the four baseball diamonds available to the public, but for the most part, our "stadium" was an overgrown field in our neighborhood next to the Hygrade silk mill. There was a large incinerator in the middle of the field where the Hygrade burned its trash. We had to negotiate a fly ball around that incinerator, being careful not to run into it when chasing down the ball. Tony Spagnoletti became tired of running around the incinerator and climbed up and stood on top of it to field the balls hit to short center field. Every time the batter fouled one off, it landed on the roof of the Hygrade mill, and the game was halted until one of us climbed the roof to retrieve the ball. We had one ball, so that was our only recourse.

The ball itself was stained green from the tall grass and usually missing a few stitches. Occasionally, someone showed up with a brand-new baseball, and we were able to see it when it was hit into the overgrown grass! By the third or fourth inning, the new ball took on the aura of the grass, and as dusk began to settle over the neighborhood, the game would have to be called due to the inability of the fielders to see the baseball. Nobody wanted to chance getting drilled in the head by a screaming line drive!

When we took a break during the game I ran across the street for some water. Dad used to keep an empty bottle of prune juice filled with cold water in the refrigerator, and I would take it back over to the field for everyone to share a swallow or two. One day, when one of the guys finished the last bit of water, instead of handing the bottle back to me, he threw it on the roof of the silk mill. The bottle crashed through a window and landed in pieces in one of the large silk looms. By the time the employees shut down the loom, over a hundred feet of silk was ruined, and the machine had to be shut down for repairs. Within minutes, the owner of the mill was outside, and it took him less than a minute to let us know we were banished from the field. The following summer, the field was over-grown and quite an eyesore. City officials informed the owner that he needed to maintain the field properly or receive a fine. We made a deal with him, telling him we would clean up the trash and keep the field mowed if he allowed us to use it for baseball again. He agreed with one stipulation....no glass bottles allowed! We had our field back!

Summer was all about baseball for us, even when we went to the Jordan Pool for an afternoon swim. The Jordan Pool, like the other city pools at the time, had a large area of sand located at the far end of the fenced in pool area. It was there that the national pastime continued. We would select an old soda cup from the trash, crumble it into a ball, and take over the sand area. Scratching out bases in the sand, we chose sides, and using our hand as a bat, began another game of baseball. Eventually, one of the lifeguards would walk down, confiscate our soda cup, and send us back to the pool. It seems that the parents of little children weren't too pleased seeing their little ones trying to share the "big sandbox" with "those ruffians"!

Even the summer mornings were dominated by baseball. We would sit on my porch and play games using our beloved Topps baseball cards. Every kid had a box of cards or, at the very least, a wad of them wrapped carefully with a rubber band. I remember buying five packs of cards at a time for the outrageous price of five cents a pack and throwing the gum away. The gum was a thin pink rectangle containing absolutely no flavor at all and usually harder than the baseball cards contained in the pack. We played a game in which we tossed the cards against the wall and somehow either won or lost our card, or we simply just traded cards... each guy believing he made the better deal. Years later, I remember walking through a street in Cooperstown, home of the Baseball Hall of Fame, and seeing a sign in one of the memorabilia shops which read, "We have the baseball cards your Mom threw away."

Once or twice every summer, we would be lucky enough to

travel to Philadelphia to watch our beloved Phillies play at Connie Mack Stadium. It was a rare treat indeed, and we enjoyed every minute of it, regardless of the fact that the Phillies were awful! We sat with our dads and watched as Willy "Puddin Head" Jones, Harry "The Horse" Anderson and the rest of the team wallowed in futility. Guys like Richie Ashburn and Robin Roberts were our heroes. At night, I would put my portable radio, adorned with the faces of Phillies players, under my pillow and listen to every inning of every game.

Today's stadiums are magnificent edifices with gigantic scoreboards, restaurants, and prescription turf fields. These are far different from Breadon Field, home to the Allentown Cardinals. Aptly named, it was a "field" rather than a stadium. Dad and I, along with Tony and his Dad, attended Cardinals games at the field and sat on wooden benches to watch our home-town heroes battle the Williamsport Grays or some other obscure Minor League team on a diamond not much better than the fields on which we played at the local Allentown parks.

Breadon Field was purchased by Max Hess, owner of Allentown's largest department store, and re-named Max Hess Stadium. There were a few upgrades, but, for the most part, the stadium remained intact. It was the home of the Allentown Red Sox, the Minor League affiliate of the Boston Red Sox. We were all issued a free "knothole" pass from our teachers at the end of the school year- courtesy of Max Hess. We sat in bleachers in the outfield and watched players like Zeke King and Tracy Stallard lead the A-sox to the Minor League pennant.

I would be remiss if I didn't take a moment to mention a bit of trivia here. Tracy Stallard was our best pitcher and went on to pitch for the Boston Red Sox. Naturally, we were very excited to see our hometown hero pitching in the majors! Unfortunately, Tracy's claim to fame (or infamy) came toward the end of the 1961 season when he surrendered Roger Maris's 61st homerun, breaking Babe Ruth's long-standing record!

Despite all these venues and Major and Minor League ball players, our biggest kick still came from watching the Italian Club team play on the first diamond at Jordan Park. Men from the Italian Club would bring lawn chairs and set them up on the railroad tracks behind the field while we usually sat or stood behind the backstop at home plate to watch the game. Guys like Arnie Plessel, Bobby Kurtz, and Zeke Delong were our heroes, and we loved watching them play. Tony and I were given the honor of passing the hat among the crowd. These guys weren't getting paid huge sums of money, but they enjoyed a little "beer money" to spend at the I-Club after the game. We were rewarded for our efforts with official IC baseball hats. I cherished my I-Club hat and wore it religiously all summer.

3.

Street Games

The streets were a perfect venue for other games such as "kick the can," "dog and deer," and "three feet off the mud gutter." Every kid in the neighborhood turned out after dark for a spirited game of "flashlight tag." The sidewalks were decorated with multiple versions of hopscotch courts, and we could always count on Mr. Russo, the local shoe repairman, to provide us with an unending supply of "hoppy heels." A deck of playing cards and a few of Mom's clothes pins were all that were needed to transform our bikes into motorcycles. Using the clothes pins, we fastened the cards to the wheels in such a way that the spokes caused them to flap as they passed over them. We usually began with one or two cards on each wheel, but before long, we were up to five or six cards, turning our relatively "quiet" neighborhood into the Daytona 500!

Small, family owned markets scattered throughout our neighborhood provided us with a plethora of exciting goodies and gadgets. We flew our GoHi balsa wood airplanes in fields and parking lots and tossed our cap rockets into the air in the neighborhood streets. These tiny rockets were made of rubber and plastic with a steel firing pin in the front. After unscrewing the top of the rocket and inserting a cap inside, we launched the plastic missiles into the air. When the firing pin struck the street, it detonated the cap creating a harmless bang. Harmless enough? Sure, at least until we decided to improvise. If one cap provided a bang, we had to know how many caps could be jammed inside. Soon, these innocuous little toys were exploding with such force, the tops were being blown off!

In today's litigious society, overly-protective parents wouldn't consider sending their children outside without a bike helmet. The thought of their loved ones running around with a sixteen-inch tube of hard plastic in their mouths would send even the most liberal parent into a panic. We enjoyed such a toy! Pea shooters were nothing more than a twenty-five-cent plastic tube used to launch hard, dried peas which we stored by the dozens inside our mouth. If one suffered the misfortune of falling forward during a pea shooter battle, he or she ran the risk of swallowing the mouth full of peas or perhaps having the plastic tube imbed itself into the roof of his or her mouth!

Just about every red-blooded boy growing up in towns across America in the 1950's and '60s was the recipient of that most prized and cherished possession known as a Daisy BB gun. Before sending us into the civilized world armed with our "Daisies." our parents gave us the obligatory lecture. "This is not a toy" began the talk from our dads. We were taught not to "point your weapons at anyone," not to shoot at birds, and all the lessons of proper gun handling.

Every kid with whom I grew up spent a fair portion of his allowance on plastic model kits. Models of cars and airplanes sat on shelves in our bedrooms next to battleships, animals, and even famous people. For some inexplicable reason, I gathered all the models which my dad and I painstakingly glued and painted over the course of several years, took them out into our back yard and placed them strategically among my mother's prized rose bushes where I proceeded to blast them to smithereens with my trusted Daisy BB gun!

This may be construed as the act of a future terrorist; however, in truth, it was nothing more than a bored thirteen-year old who thought it seemed like a good idea at the time. Unfortunately, Dad and I weren't on the same page with that idea. Old Daisy and I parted ways that day, and I have never fired another weapon to this day!

4.

Pots and Ponies

Once a week during the summer months, various local farmers with a truckload of fresh produce drove along our street shouting a very familiar word that brought our moms bolting through the screen doors armed with their purses. "Huckster!" the farmer called out while he and members of his family placed fresh vegetables in brown, paper bags as coins clinked between him and our moms.

The huckster was usually followed by the street cleaner. A huge tank truck rumbled through the neighborhood as it sprayed water from jets, washing everything to the curb. We quickly removed our PF Flyers and dashed into the street. It didn't matter to us that the spray kicked up dirt and debris from the street, and the gloppy mess attached itself to our legs and clothing.

Another neighborhood fixture was the pony man. He turned up every year leading a tired-looking pony that wanted nothing more than to be grazing in some cool pasture. Armed with his black tripod camera and a few articles of western gear, the pony man set up on our sidewalk. After donning a well-worn cowboy hat, a set of chaps, and a scarf, I was placed on the saddle. Immortalized in black and white, I dismounted, and my sister took the reins. By noon, every kid on our block possessed an identical photograph. Most of us still have those photos today.

The familiar clang of the umbrella man's bell was heard throughout the neighborhood every few weeks. He held this title because one of his specialties was repairing umbrellas. He carried a sack of tools and somehow managed to walk through our neighborhood with a pedal-powered grinding wheel complete with a seat slung over his shoulder. He sharpened knives and scissors using his wheel and repaired pots and pans as well as lamps and other appliances with tools from his pouch. He charged whatever price he felt to be fair, and it was not unusual for him to settle for a glass of whiskey or homemade Italian wine.

Every summer Dad chose a pleasant evening to set up his movie screen at the far end of the yard. He then placed his 8mm movie projector on our back porch. Everyone in the row came out into their yards, sat on lawn chairs, blankets, or their porch steps and readied themselves with popcorn and Kool-Aid for the show.

We watched cartoons and Abbott and Costello shorts under the stars. The movies were in black and white and the film contained no sound. It didn't matter to our neighbors that they were unable to read the dialogue at the bottom of the screen. Nobody seemed to care. We were all outside, under the stars, eating popcorn and having a good time.

When the show ended, everyone applauded, said "good night," and headed into their homes. My friend, Ed, and I helped my dad take down the screen and put away the projector before setting up my Pecos Bill tent in our back yard. Ed and I listened to the Phillies game on my radio and played cards before calling it a night and sleeping under a summer moon. Life was good!

Riding the range on the sidewalks of Jordan Street.

Still riding in Utah with a supersized horse!

5.

Hey Kids, What Time Is it?

When I was seven years old, something happened in our home that had a lasting effect on our family for years to come. Dad and my uncle carried a most unusual piece of furniture into our basement. I should point out that, unlike the rest of the basements in our row, ours had walls of knotty pine, a tile floor, and was completely furnished. It included a magnificent bar with a sink and a back bar containing pictures and shelves displaying my mom's bowling trophies as well as other memorabilia. Our entire basement was fashioned by the hands of my dad, who may have been a baker by trade, but was one of the most skillful carpenters I have ever known. Dad and my uncle placed this new piece of furniture on a cabinet built by Dad for this purpose.

After plugging this object into one of the receptacles on the wall, my dad turned a knob on the box, and a white, snowy picture appeared on the glass window. Suddenly, my excitement began to diminish. We had plenty of lamps in our basement already, and I didn't even think this oversized lamp provided enough light by which to read. Having lost all enthusiasm for this contraption, I headed outside to play with my friends. Strolling through our yard, I was drawn to the sound of voices and tools coming from the roof. My Dad and uncle were assembling what appeared to be some sort of tree made of metal. Should I ask? I decided that I had enough surprises for that day.

It was about a half hour until dinner, and I was sitting in our basement staring at this strange box with the bright snowy window when suddenly something like a target appeared on the screen. It had a large number 3 in the center, and a constant buzzing emanated from the box. Fascinated, I just sat there staring. The face of a man dressed in a strange outfit appeared on the screen and spoke the words that forever changed my life! "Hey, kids, what time is it?" I was frozen to my chair as Buffalo Bob led the Peanut Gallery in a rousing version of "It's Howdy Doody Time." Frantically, I called my sister and my parents to "come and see this!" When the show ended, the target, which I learned from my dad, was a "test pattern," returned for a few hours before something called Frontier Playhouse appeared on the screen.

It didn't take long for word to spread throughout the neighborhood. Suddenly, kids began to show up at our front door just before five o'clock, and the sound of a dozen voices could be heard singing "It's Howdy Doody Time."

Our parents had to rearrange the dinner hour around the Howdy Doody Show, but nobody in the neighborhood seemed to care. My Nonna, our Italian grandmother, didn't speak a word of English, yet she never missed an episode of Frontier Playhouse. Her favorite cowboy was Hopalong Cassidy, or as she called him, "Hopalong Casadeech."

My dad loved his shows, but it bothered him that they were all broadcast in black and white. Upon returning from the hardware store, he sequestered himself in his workshop each afternoon after returning from the bakery. He finally emerged from his workshop one evening carrying a huge wheel with sheets of cellophane in various colors. The wheel was attached to a motor, and when he plugged it in, it began to spin. I'm not sure what was supposed to happen, but the result was a cacophony of ear-splitting sounds accompanied by a screen filled with static. Dad was good, but not that good! It was years before the NBC Peacock flashed on TV screens announcing, "This program is being brought to you in living color."

6.

Let's All Go To The Movies!

Sundays in our neighborhood meant church, but it was also "movie day." Almost every kid in our part of town could be found standing in line at the Franklin Theater waiting for the doors to open. Never missing an opportunity to make a sale, the balloon man would work the crowd with his long, skinny balloons, twisting them into various animal shapes while we watched in amazement.

By the time the doors opened, our pockets were filled with balloons as we filed into the theater. Admission to the movies cost fifteen cents for children under thirteen years of age. Because I was an unusually tall kid, my mom always sent me to the show with my birth certificate to avoid having to pay the adult price.

Loaded down with Jujubes, Raisinets, and Necco wafers, we headed to our seats ready for the show. Following the Movietone Newsreel, a few cartoons preceded the latest episode of Flash Gordon or The Green Hornet. I now realize the brilliant marketing of those serials. We were more interested in the next episode of the serial than we were about the feature presentation!

Double features were part of every Sunday's programming much to the delight of our parents who enjoyed an afternoon of peace and quiet. That tranquility was extended for them since nobody cleared the theater at the end of the first show. We just sat there and watched everything again!

Sunday might have meant "movie day" most of the time; however, if Mom and Dad were in a traveling mood, the entire family piled into our 1952 Ford Customliner to take part in that most popular adventure of the 1950's - the "Sunday Drive." "Where to?" one might ask, but as my father always told us, "It's not the destination, but the journey." Off we went, Mom and Dad in the front seat while my brother, sister and I jammed into the rear of the car as we began our "journey" to nowhere in particular. Choosing a road or highway, we headed out of the neighborhood, and eventually, past the city limits of Allentown. One day we would travel through rural countryside, stopping briefly for Mom to gather dried milkweed pods or other exotic plants found in the wild suburbs of Allentown. On another occasion, the red Customliner found its way to the Poconos. Once there, we would park and gaze in awe at the waterfalls, the same waterfalls we had seen on many of our Sunday drives in the past! If the rising price of gasoline served any positive purpose, it put the kibosh on our Sunday drives, and we were reunited with Flash Gordon and The Green Lantern.

Like all automobiles in the 1950s, our Ford Customliner was adorned with a hood ornament. These elaborate works of art graced the hood of every brand of car. Sculpted in fine chrome and stainless steel, they came in the form of winged goddesses, gazelles, jungle animals and even snails! Our Ford sported a large chrome swan, its wings spread, primed for take-off.

On certain days when I returned from a day at the pool, it only required a quick glance at Dad's car to know a special evening was planned. The swan was missing from the front of our Ford! We were going to the drive-in! Dad always removed the swan from our car so the family could view the screen.

Mom loaded our pillows and pajamas into the already cramped back seat, and off we went. We had no idea what movies were playing that night, but it really didn't matter to us. We were going to the drive-in! As soon as Dad parked the Ford on one of the inclines and hung our speaker on the car window, we were out of the car and on our way to the playground. Spinning around at breakneck speed on one of the playground rides as our dinner came precariously close to the surface, we kept one eye on the screen.

Suddenly, Tom and Jerry flashed onto the huge screen, and every kid bolted from the playground in a mad rush to their parents' car!

By the end of the first movie, my siblings and I, bleary-eyed and cramped, were given a few dollars to head to the snack bar. A funny looking elf appeared on the screen during the intermission. He proceeded to dine on every item available at the snack bar and dabbed his face with a napkin between every bite. He then reached over to the clock on the screen and pulled the minute hand down one number to let us know how many minutes were left until the second show.

As the elf moved the hand down to the final minute, it was time for us to change into our pajamas. Sometime during the second feature, Dad removed the speaker and quietly left the drive-in. We, of course, were sound asleep in the back seat by then. It took me a few years until I took my own children to the drive-in to realize that my parents could have cared less about the second feature. They were simply waiting for us to fall asleep!

7.

Set The Night On Fire

In addition to our bakery and luncheonette, my parents owned the apartments above the shop. Most of the tenants were great people who took care of the property and paid their rent on time. Unfortunately, one family had two boys that made my dad's life miserable. In addition to trashing the apartment, they used the walls for target practice with their BB guns. Finally, Dad had to ask them to leave, and things quieted down, or so we thought.

One night about three o'clock in the morning, Dad heard someone shouting outside his bedroom window. He was awakened by stones hitting his window. He looked out and saw one of his drivers standing on the sidewalk below, calling to him and waving his hands. Dad rushed downstairs and opened the front door to find Wimpy standing there. Wimpy was a jolly guy who acquired his nickname because of his uncanny resemblance to the hamburger eating character in Popeye cartoons, however, he was anything but jolly that night.

"One of the trucks is on fire!" he shouted.

My dad threw on his clothes and ran the two blocks down the street to the bakery to discover the truck fully engulfed in flames! Wimpy had already called the fire department, and they arrived a few minutes later to quell the blaze.

Nothing was left of the panel truck but a charred, empty shell. When the police examined the inside of the truck, they found several hand grenades lying on the floor. Everyone was quite alarmed until Wimpy informed my dad and the police that they were duds that he had purchased at an Army Navy store as souvenirs. The truck was a total loss, and my dad had a pretty good idea who was responsible, but he was never able to prove any wrong doing.

A few nights later, my sister and I walked past the bakery with our two cousins on our way to a cartoon festival at the Franklin Theater. My cousin was one of those guys who just had a way of doing the wrong thing at the wrong time. As we passed by the alley where the truck was parked, my cousin Ron climbed inside, released the emergency brake, and pretended to drive. The alley led into the parking lot of the Italian Club, and the parking lot ended at a rather steep embankment overlooking the street below. The next morning my family was returning from church by way of that street, and, as we passed the club's parking lot, we saw the burned-out truck teetering on the edge of the embankment, ready to plunge down onto the street below! Dad quickly pulled our car over and ran up the embankment. He pushed the truck back and put on the emergency brake.

I know my dad suspected that the same people who burned the truck were responsible for releasing the emergency brake, but my sister and I know differently. The truck didn't fall onto the street, and nobody was hurt, so we figured it was best to just let it be our secret.

8.

Benches and Snakes

Everyone in our Italian neighborhood attended mass at our Lady of Mount Carmel Italian Church. Our group of guys arrived at church in Ritchie's '52 Chevy and sat together in one pew. As much as we tried to behave, talk about last night's movie or someone's hot date seemed to attract the attention of the nuns sitting a few rows behind us.

During the mass, the nuns would instruct a few of the adult faithful to "bring out the benches"! We all dreaded the sight of the green benches being placed on both sides of the alter. One of the nuns would approach our pew and take whoever was unlucky enough to be seated at the end of the row by the ear. She then led the entire group to the alter to sit on those awful benches.

The priest patiently stopped his sermon until we were all seated. We then had to endure the angry stares of the elderly Italian ladies, clutching their rosaries like assault rifles! To make matters worse, I could see my mom and dad looking at me with that "wait until you get home" glare in their eyes.

Forking over a cool tweny-five cents to the clerk at MCrory's Five and Dime, I carefully placed my new bow tie in the bag and headed home. The tie was brown with white dots and featured a long, plastic tube with a rubber bulb attached to its end. When the bulb was pressed, a column of air rushed through the tube into the bow tie causing a rather hideous snake to protrude outside the tie. As my family dressed for church. I donned my new tie, carefully slipping the plastic tube through the sleeve of my shirt until the rubber bulb fit into the palm of my hand. The stage was set.

In the middle of the priest's sermon, I carefully squeezed the bulb. Out popped the snake, his beady eyes and rubber fang gazing at an elderly Italian woman seated next to me. Her blood-curdling scream sounded throughout the tiny congregation! When we got home, my bowtie, along with its rubber occupant, was immediately tossed into the trash, and I spent the next two hours composing my letter of apology to our priest.

I was sternly reminded I would not be missing confession the following Saturday. That confession turned out to be quite memorable. Tony and I were walking home from confession when Tony happened to see our two buddies, Chas and Gerry, on the other side of the street on their way to confession. Gerry is a little guy, but one of the toughest people I ever met. In fact, he held the record at our high school for pinning his opponent in thirteen seconds – a record that lasted for many years. Spotting Gerry on the other side of the street, Tony said to me, "Why don't you sing Shrimp Boats Are A-Comin"? It was a very popular song at the time.

I broke out into song. Gerry charged across the street, jumped on my back, and began to pummel me! My dear friend, Tony, threw me under the bus that day. I think it was my penance for scaring the lady with my snake!

9.

Goodnight, Irene

When my dad and uncle were still partners in the bakery, they pooled their money and purchased twenty-seven acres of land in the country. What makes this a story about the neighborhood is the fact that so many of our neighbors became invested in this land. Their investment did not come in the form of dollars, but rather their time.

We loved our Italian neighborhood, but the idea to leave the streets and factories for a few days a week to enjoy the fresh air of the country was very appealing. Everyone joined together like one big family to build a cottage on the land, rich with fields of strawberries, a stream shaded by tall trees and teeming with fish.

After finishing their day at the bakery, Dad and my uncle packed up their tools and headed to their property in the country. They were joined there by friends and neighbors of every age to work on the house. While the men labored in the warm sun, my sister and I, along with our two cousins, played in the stream, caught crayfish, and helped our moms pick strawberries. Neighbors cleared the land, gathered for birthday parties and picnics and worked to finish the house.

At the end of the day, everyone washed up and took a seat at the long table built by my dad. My mom and Nonna joined the other ladies in preparing a huge feast. Since the house wasn't completed, they cooked over camp stoves put together by the men. For kids living every day in the city, sitting under the trees in the cool country air was paradise!

One of the camp stoves was covered with a sheet of steel and was used for cooking. My Zio Tony would gather crayfish from the stream and toss them on the "griddle." They scurried around and eventually flipped upside down, cooked to a crisp. Tony would pluck them from the stove and pop them into his mouth, shells and all, like he was eating popcorn!

During the weekend, many of us stayed at the house. By that time, the house was under roof and contained a rudimentary kitchen, complete with running water and a stove. We slept on old sofas and army cots while the men went out with flashlights and mallets to walk the stream. As the morning sun rose, the men trudged back to the house carrying a large bushel basket filled with frogs. The women spent the day preparing the frogs while Dad and the rest of the neighbors continued working on the house. Dinner that night consisted of breaded frog's legs with fresh strawberries and cream for dessert.

My cousin Ron and I relaxing on the cottage steps.

One of the more colorful characters from the neighborhood and a relative of my aunt's was a man by the name of Mickey Amato. He was a former prisoner of war during World War II, and quite a character. He set up a tent in the large field and had all the kids find a sturdy tree branch to use as a rifle. He would then lead us

Dad and Bugsy working on the cottage.

in a charge against the invisible enemy. We enjoyed our afternoons with "General Mickey."

The weekend always ended with a huge bonfire. We roasted marshmallows and sang songs while the adults drank homemade wine in front of the roaring blaze. My fondest memory of those campfires was listening to my dad as he sang "Goodnight Irene, I'll see you in my dreams" in front of the dwindling flames.

Wth the fire safely extinguished, we loaded our cars and headed back to civilization. It was truly a beautiful chapter in my life, and I regret that it ended way too soon!

10.

The Best Bread In Town

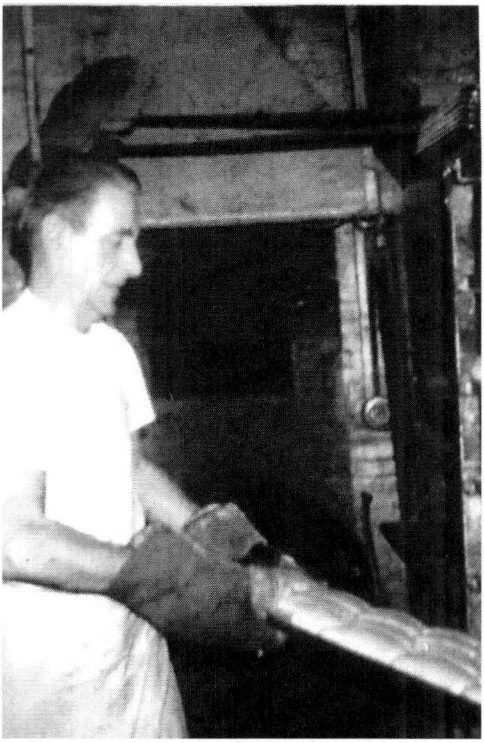

Dad loading another batch of hot rolls on the cooking rack.

Situated behind the Allentown Italian Club and separated by a tiny alley with the unlikely name of Carrot Street sat my father's Italian bakery. It was an old, brick and stone building with a coal bin adorning its outside facade. To the right of the entrance, stood a metal cooling rack which was the only structure that indicated a bakery was inside. The front of the building contained a small luncheonette, also a part of our combined families. The luncheonette offered many of our neighbors a place to congregate, inside as well as out front on warm, summer evenings where talk of sports, upcoming events at the I-Club, work, or even the latest gossip took place.

I remember working in the bakery with my cousins alongside my dad and My Zio Top. Dad and Top worked side by side inside the little shop named Roma Bakery. It was a lively place to work. My zio was usually singing along with whatever song was playing on the radio at the time. "I'm gonna sit right down, and write myself a letter, oh, yeah"! It was the late 1950s and early 60s, and my cousins and I were young teenagers at the time.

Our house was just a few blocks away, so I could walk to work in the summertime or on weekends during the school year. My dad began his day around four a.m., opening the shop and shoveling a wheelbarrow or two of coal and loading it into the long, stone hearth oven. Next, came the first mix... two hundred pounds of flour along with the bricks of yeast, malt, salt and water all loaded into the Triumph dough mixer. Other mixes came later in the morning. All the bread was made by hand at the work table. Steak rolls, hoagie rolls, Vienna loaves, sesame loaves, unique breads known as star loaves because of the resemblance to stars were all made at the work table. The most popular loaf of bread was the coronet. Our customers, most of them Italians, referred to the coronets as "cornittis." They were made by rolling two sides of the dough tightly and twisting them until they resembled an airplane. I really don't know how else to describe one. Besides my cousins and me, other young men from the neighborhood like Gussy and Clem worked in the bakery at various times. We worked fast because the hundreds of pounds of dough on the table needed to be fashioned into loaves and loaded into the ovens before the dough rose too much. I remember taking a stick of butter from our refrigerator before heading to the bakery. When the first rolls came out of the oven and were placed on the cooling rack, I tore one open and loaded it with butter. There was nothing better than one of those hot, steaming rolls with butter melting inside!

Our customers included local restaurants and grocery stores who bought our bread, but we also had regular "walk-in" customers, most of whom lived in the neighborhood. They were the Italians who had come here from the old country and lived in the same homes all their lives. There was Gigi DeMarki, who came in every day, picked up one of our large bags and began filling it with several loaves of bread. He then proceeded to place a dime on the work table. My dad turned his bag upside down, dumped most of the bread back out, and settled for his dime. Dewey Trenge came in every morning at approximately eleven o'clock for his one loaf of star bread. Dewey created handmade neckties from silk and always brought us new neckties at Christmas time. So, it went throughout the course of the day, people from the neighborhood walking in to get their bread and bringing with them a bottle of homemade wine or a salami they had cured in their basement. Next to the buttered roll, there was nothing tastier than tearing off a piece of the salami and putting it in one of the rolls!

One of the rights of passage for the guys in the neighborhood, having acquired their driver's licenses, was to drive one of our delivery trucks either to the restaurants or the local stores. It was heaven for these guys, as it was for me when I eventually turned sixteen, to not only get to drive a delivery truck, all standard shift, of course, but to be paid to do it.

One day, I rode with my dad on one of our delivery routes along with my cousin, who had just acquired his learner's permit. Since my cousin only had a permit, he required a licensed driver to be in the vehicle with him. We had pulled up behind a car double parked on the street, and after a few minutes, my dad called to the driver to move his vehicle. A shouting match ensued between my dad and the driver, who steadfastly refused to move his car. Finally, my dad told my cousin to back up and go around him. Unfortunately, my cousin, thinking the truck was in reverse, stepped on the gas and plowed into the rear of the man's car just as the man's passenger, using his cane, was getting out of the car! He wasn't injured; however, the driver was never convinced my cousin didn't ram into his car on purpose. So much for learning to drive a standard shift!

Every so often, Big John would arrive in his black limousine. His "men" would get out first and Big John would enter the bakery surrounded by these guys. He was always dressed in black from head to toe, and it always amused me to watch the flour settling on his black overcoat! He selected his bread, and always insisted on paying for it even though my dad and zio told him it was "on the house." One day John picked me up in his limousine and took me to his house. He asked me to put up his Christmas lights and then had his driver return me to the bakery. A few days later, he returned to the bakery for his bread and told me to join him in the back of the car. We drove to a local clothing factory, and John said to the manager, "The kid is gonna pick out some suits." After selecting a few suits, I was told to "go back and get a couple sport coats." Afterwards, we left with no money changing hands. I didn't ask any questions!

Our family also ran a luncheonette in front of the bakery. My aunts and uncles took turns behind the counter alongside my mom making steak sandwiches and hamburgers, hot dogs and milkshakes for the workers from the textile factory across the street. I remember the happy sounds of the jukebox and the pinball machines as well as the laughter of the patrons who gathered for lunch or just some conversation and fellowship. Occasionally, I slipped away from the bakery to play a game or two on the pinball machine, but my dad wasted no time letting me know I was "on the clock" in the bakery!

My first job in the luncheonette was scraping the old chewing gum from beneath the counter and putting it into an empty, five-gallon ice-cream drum. For that, I received a nickel, which I promptly put into the pinball machine. Occasionally, my dad walked my sister and me to the luncheonette in the evening after it was closed and we all made huge ice-cream sundaes. All the men from the neighborhood hung out in front of the restaurant and talked, laughed, and socialized.

In the early sixties, my Zio Top retired from the bakery and moved into the apartment above the bakery. By then, the luncheonette was closed, and my zio opened a ceramic shop in its place. I was just about to graduate from high school, and my dad asked me if I could give him "one year" of my life to help him get the shop running smoothly. That was the beginning of a very close time with my dad. He and I worked side by side in the bakery, and I really got to know him for the first time. I got to a point where I could anticipate his every move in that shop, and I was one step ahead of his having to tell me what he wanted me to do next. The day after my dad's mother died, I walked into the bakery and saw my dad sitting on a box, crying. It was the only time in my life I ever saw him cry. That year is, and always will be, one of the most important years of my life. It was the year I became more than just my dad's son. I became his friend.

That year, I began to deliver the first route of the day. One of the stores on our first route was the A&P supermarket. As I began unloading the baskets of bread from the truck, people gathered around me and took the bread from the baskets before I had the chance to load the bread onto the shelves inside the store. I told them I had to check the bread in with the manager first, but they told me they were afraid they wouldn't be able to get the bread once inside the store. Our bread was that good! The manager of the A&P told the customers they had to wait until he checked the bread in, but they couldn't wait that long. He finally gave up and just let them take the bread right to the checkout counter.

Two notable events occurred that year that totally amazed me about my dad. A representative of Freihofer's Bakery, one of the largest companies in Allentown at the time, entered our shop and told Dad that he was authorized to offer him $50,000 for his recipe with one stipulation: Dad would have to close the shop and not make any more bread. I was blown away! Fifty thousand dollars was quite a considerable sum in those days, and I was already spending some of the money in my mind. Dad turned him down flat, and although I was shocked and frustrated with him that day, my respect for him, if possible, grew even greater.

The other event was a bit more comical. A reporter walked into the bakery and told my dad that our local newspaper wanted to do a story about him as the last of the "one man" bakeries that still existed in Allentown in the 1960's. Once again, as I prepared to make sure the man spelled my name correctly in the newspaper, Dad said to him, "I just got out of prison, and I'm trying to keep a low profile." The reporter stared at him, turned, and left the shop. Once again, when I thought the man could not amaze me anymore, he blew me away!

One of my friends joined us on weekends and in the summer and eventually he took over the first delivery route for me which enabled me to remain in the shop with my dad. He installed an eight-track tape player (remember those?) into one of our trucks. He was really into his music those days, and still is today. One morning, he spent ten minutes in the truck organizing his tapes and music for the route before heading out to make his deliveries. As my dad and I were preparing the next load of bread, he turned to me with a look of astonishment on his face.

"Dad, what's wrong?" I asked.

"Look around," he replied. "The guy went out with an empty truck!"

I couldn't wait for his return. He had driven all the way to his first restaurant stop before realizing he had nothing in the truck. He had to drive back to the bakery and face the music – no pun intended. I had a lot of fun with that one and never let him forget it, but he was a good sport about it and we both enjoyed a good laugh.

After twenty years in that bakery without a break, my dad was beat. I told him it was time to turn the shop over to me long enough for him to take a vacation. I knew I could do what needed to be done, and I convinced him to take my mom on a two-week cruise. His shop and his livelihood were in my hands! I remember the first morning my alarm going off at three-thirty a.m. and awakening to total darkness. I never felt as totally alone as I did that morning. I walked down to the shop, shoveled the coal and fired up the hearth oven. Just as the first mix of two hundred pounds of dough was ready to come out of the mixer onto the work table, a fuse blew, and I was in total darkness.

By the time I found the fuses and got the lights back on, the dough was rising to heights never seen in that bakery! I called my friend to ask him to come in a little earlier than I planned, but he hadn't gotten home yet. The first day was a wreck, but the next two weeks went smoothly, and with the help of my friend, Dad came home to his business intact.

As my "promised year" drew to an end, my mom retired from her job as hostess at the George Washington Motor Lodge and came to work in the bakery. Mom and I had a little "deal" going when local customers came into the shop. She and I split the coins the customers gave us rather than putting them in the change bag. We referred to this as our "filch" money. My dad always pretended to be angry with us, but in truth, he enjoyed our thievery and laughed right along with us.

Eventually, I became a teacher, but still found time on weekends and summers to join my mom and dad in the bakery. In 1974, I had my first of two back surgeries. While I was in the hospital recuperating, my dad had a heart attack and was told he had to close the bakery "immediately." It seems that the flour dust in the air had gotten into his lungs over time and caused his heart to enlarge. I remember Bobby Russoli getting one of the last cornittis, spraying it with gold paint, mounting it on a plaque inscribed with the words, "World's Greatest Baker," and giving it to my dad. I held onto that gold cornitti for many years until it finally succumbed to the ravages of time.

By the time I was released from the hospital, the bakery was gone. The equipment had been sold, and there was only an empty room where so much laughter had taken place and so many wonderful people had become friends and family.

Years later, after returning from my dad's funeral, I went down to that little alley named Carrot Street and sat with my back against the wall of the Italian Club directly in front of our bakery. It was dark and empty, but I allowed myself to travel back in time to remember all the precious moments of my life which were spent there.

11.

Peach Jam

A few years after Dad and my uncle sold the bungalow, I still longed for a place to spend time away from the city and all the noise that came with it. After the sale of our land, my Zio Top bought a farm in a place by the name of Fogelsville, a sleepy, little town on the outskirts of Allentown. The town has grown since then, but at the time the countryside was dotted with farms and small country houses. After a day at the bakery, my cousin Ron and I would hop into the back of my zio's pickup truck and head out of town on the major highway leading from the city. That highway is now a quiet street with the major highway running parallel to it. Of course, everyone knows that kids ride in the back seat, secured safely in the vehicle with a seat belt, but this was a different era. Not only did we not ride in the back seat of my uncle's truck, we sat in the open bed of the truck, harnessed to nothing.

I loved my cousins, and I couldn't wait to spend two glorious weeks on their farm with them. I was a city kid, and the idea of slopping the pigs and feeding the chickens and cows was exciting to me. There were horses, wonderful, beautiful horses! My cousins and I rode them bareback in the corral and around the farm. To me it was a dream come true!

There was always something to do, and we never tired of new adventures. One night my cousin and I found two very large cardboard boxes and took them to a steep hill where we proceeded to climb inside them and roll down the hill. We climbed the hill and rode the boxes down over and over until bedtime, agreeing that we would go back there in the morning and continue the fun. After breakfast, boxes in hand, we headed back to the hill. Things appeared different in the morning light. It was then that we discovered that the hill, which seemed so soft and comfortable on the way down, was covered in poison ivy! That set my exciting adventure to my uncle's farm back about a week! Five days and a generous helping of Calamine lotion had us back on track in time for baling season.

The hay fields had been cut and baled for feed, and the bales were ready to be loaded onto my uncle's large wagon attached to his tractor. My uncle and his hired hand began loading the bales onto the wagon using hand-held hooks like those used by dock workers. When asked about hooks for us, my uncle's hired hand laughed and told us to pick the bales up by hand and carry them to the wagon. This did not sit well with my cousin who told me to "follow him" to the house. We found rods from an old TV antenna in his dad's workshop, and we bent them into the shape of hooks. It didn't seem to matter to us that there were no points on the rods to stick them into the hay bales. The only thing left to do was to attach them to handles. We drilled holes into two pieces of wood and stuck the rods through the holes. Unfortunately, there was no way to attach the rods to the wooden handles. It was then that my cousin, the same cousin who almost drove our burned-out bakery truck over the embankment of the Italian Club, decided to "weld" them together. I don't know much about welding, but I'm somewhat certain one cannot weld a piece of metal to a piece of wood!

Ron took a roll of his dad's solder and wrapped it around the rods protruding through the wooden handles. Now came the tricky part. How did one melt the solder onto the wood? Simple. Douse the solder with gasoline and apply a match! The next thing we knew, the workshop was ablaze, and my uncle's workbench was a charred mess. Scratch that idea, in fact, scratch any subsequent welding plans! Dousing the blaze with water from my aunt's laundry tub, my cousin put the entire mess into a vise until he smashed the wad of solder against the antenna rod, and we returned to the hay field. Harvey, my uncle's eighty-year old hired hand, took one look at my cousin's hook, grabbed it from his hand, and in one quick motion, pulled it apart! We spent the rest of the day carrying bales of hay to the wagon.

My Zio Top's main source of revenue on the farm was a large peach orchard filled with sweet, luscious peaches for harvest and sale. When it was time to harvest the peaches, the entire clan of relatives and neighbors from the city joined us for the task. My zio hooked up the huge wagon to the back of his tractor, filled it with bushel baskets, and we all climbed aboard. He drove the tractor to each tree, parked, and we stood in the bed of the wagon and pick peaches, loading them into the baskets. He then moved on to the next tree, and the process was repeated. This took several days and culminated with a huge feast prepared on the outdoor barbeque. Top had a roadside stand located next to the highway, and my cousins and I, along with my aunt, took turns dealing with the customers stopping by for some delicious peaches. The little stand turned out to be quite profitable, and I found the work very enjoyable.

One night while we were sleeping, we heard a terrible crash coming from the highway in front of the farmhouse. Jolted from sleep, we all ran outside to see what had happened. A huge eighteen-wheeler had run off the highway and, as luck (or bad luck) would have it, crashed into the roadside stand, crushing it. The driver wasn't badly hurt, but the stand and all the peaches were destroyed. With the peach stand gone, and the August temperatures reaching the 90's, it was time to cool off!

Life on the farm was made better once we had our own swimming pool, which my aunt's brother helped to build. He owned a construction company and one evening he came out to the farm with a large bulldozer and dug an enormous hole about two hundred feet from the house in front of a small spring. He said if we waited a few days, we would have our very own swimming pool. Sure enough, within three days the hole was filled, and we were ready for our first swim. We grabbed our bathing suits, found several tire tubes in the barn, and jumped in for our first swim! The bottom was muddy, the water cold, and there was nothing like chlorine or a filter pump, but it was a pool! About a week later, the groundhogs had burrowed so many holes into the banks of the pool that it dried up. It became a grass-covered hole in the landscape, but for one fun-filled week it was our very own swimming pool. The loss of our pool was over-shadowed by a much more traumatic experience involving my Nonna!

One of the more popular things to do at Easter time was to go to downtown Allentown and buy either an Easter chick or duck at Woolworths. I had chosen a duck and named him Quackers, while my sister, Anita, opted for a blue chick. The chicks were injected with food dye and came out of their eggs in a dazzling array of colors. Fortunately, such a practice is no longer permitted and livestock is no longer sold in drugstores!

My duck began to grow too large for our house in Allentown, so I took it to my Zio Top's farm and put him in with the other chickens and ducks in my uncle's hen house. My duck grew to adulthood, and I could visit him while staying at the farm. One night my mom and dad came to visit me at the farm, and they brought my Nonna along. We were all going to have dinner together before my family returned to the city. I walked to the hen house with my Nonna, thinking we were going to visit my duck. When we got there, she went in, took a paring knife from her apron and cut my Quackers' head off! I don't think I was ever in a state of shock as severe as that in my entire life! Please understand, this was a farm, and that is what these birds were raised for, but at that point in my life I could not believe that my Nonna could do such a thing, and in front of me! My duck was on the dinner table that night, and I will tell you that I did not eat a bite of my dinner. I am a grown man now, and I have had duck at restaurants many times, but that evening was all about a young boy seeing his pet sacrificed for dinner!

I loved my Nonna, and I understand that, in her world growing up on a farm, there was nothing wrong with what she did. In fact, I'm sure that, had she known the circumstances at the time, she would have chosen another chicken or duck for dinner.

My favorite time on that farm came in the evening. My cousins and I drove to the local ice cream stand and picked up sundaes for everyone. We all sat together in the living room with our ice cream and watched the Phillies play baseball on a little black and white television set. Afterwards, we headed to bed and listened to the sounds of the crickets chirping as cool, country air drifted in through our bedroom windows.

12.

The I-Club

Centrally located in our neighborhood and the focal point of just about everyone's life was the Allentown Italian Club. The tan brick building stood tall next to our bakery and across the street from Russoli's Italian market and was an integral part of our community. Although there were thousands of social members over the years, the I-Club truly belonged to the men and women of our neighborhood who worked and socialized there daily. Italian immigrants founded the Allentown Italian Club in 1887, and history tells us that sometime in the 1920s Mafia associates supposedly sprayed bullets in the shape of a cross into a man there. At least that's the story that was told by my mom who claims her uncles were there at the time.

The original building contained clay bocce alleys in the basement, which were the site of many intense games of bocce. In addition, the basement contained bowling alleys next to the bocce courts. In 1951, a new addition was added to the back-side of the building. The addition contained modern bowling facilities along with a nightclub and bar. This was the beginning of the heyday of the club. Local bands performed at the nightclub on Saturday nights, and because the club was a private organization, it was not subject to the blue laws of the time. Consequently, the club could serve alcohol on Sunday evenings. Because other publicly owned bars were not permitted to serve alcohol on Sunday, the Italian Club was the hottest spot in town on a Sunday night. Bands played, people danced and drank, and the club thrived!

After attending Mass every Sunday at nearby Our Lady of Mount Carmel Italian Church, the men, dressed in their best suits, would head to the club, lining up three or four deep at the bar for drinks and conversation.

Hanging outside the Italian Club.

When I was a boy, it seemed like every Saturday night we went to the club for a wedding. I just thought that was what one did on a Saturday night. I remember walking up the long, wide stairway to the banquet hall where so many young, Italian couples celebrated the beginning of their journey.

A good time was had by all as the ladies danced the polka with each other while their husbands sat at the tables drinking shots of V-O, in their words, "Wee O"! Since we were much too young to drink and certainly had little interest in dancing, we ran around the dance floor in the large hall and slid on our knees across the sand that was sprinkled on the floor to facilitate those inclined to dance. Since we were all wearing our "Sunday best," our parents were not exactly thrilled with the condition of our dress pants by the end of the evening.

I always got a kick out of watching my zios stroll up to the wedding table and fill the pockets of their sport coats with Italian wedding cookies on display at either end of the table. One hasn't lived until he or she has tasted a true wedding cookie! My Zio Buggsy was the most innovative of all my uncles. He would line the pockets of his suit with plastic bags before filling them with cookies. Since we all lived within walking distance of the club, he would walk home, empty his pockets, and return for a refill.

The time came for everyone to dance with the bride. She usually held a satin bag while she danced, and every one of the Italian men and women walked up and put money into her bag before dancing with her. That dance always reminds me of the wedding scene in the movie *Goodfellas*. During the wedding dance, Karen leaves the satin bag on a table. She turns to Henry and tells him she is a "bit concerned" about the money bag. Henry laughs and says to her, "Karen, trust me, nobody's gonna steal that bag in this room!"

There were always those "special nights": macaroni night, chicken night, and spaghetti night. The women from the Ladies' Auxiliary worked tirelessly during the day making sauce, boiling pasta, cooking meatballs, and roasting chickens in the ovens at my dad's bakery in preparation for the evening feast. This not only brought the neighborhood people out, but people from all over the city and beyond to partake in the chow. These nights were the most popular events at the I-Club. Everyone gathered at the long tables, meticulously set by the ladies that afternoon, and awaited the festivities. Various "dignitaries" sat at the tables located along the front of the stage, and speeches were made before everyone pledged our flag and sang "God Bless America." Large bowls of pasta, salad, and chicken were brought to the tables along with rolls from our bakery and pitchers of wine and water, and the sound of laughter filled the big hall. After dinner, bottles of whiskey were placed on the table, and everyone enjoyed an evening filled with laughter and dancing.

Every year a special Sunday was set aside for the Ladies' Christmas party. All the kids would gather with their parents, usually our moms, in the large banquet hall for refreshments and await the arrival of Santa Claus. The men could usually be found in the smaller banquet room sidled up to the bar, enjoying a beverage and conversation while the kids ran around in the other room. Eventually, Santa arrived with his sack and things really got frantic! Each kid walked up to Santa and received a stocking filled with goodies and a toy, furnished by our parents. We spent the afternoon playing with the toys and eating everything that wasn't "good" for us! As the day wound down, and we began to grow weary, Louie Spagnoletti set up his movie projector. We sat on the floor and watched cartoons and Our Gang comedies before walking home with our treasures.

One of the best I-Club days of the year took place miles from the city at Russoli's bungalow. To many of us, it was as special as Christmas Day and just as much (or more) fun! That special day was the Ladies Club picnic. It was held in the little town of Vera Cruz. On that day, our Italian neighborhood became a ghost town because everyone was at the picnic. Any burglar would have had a field day in our neighborhood! Every family had a "favorite spot" to set up their chairs and tables. One knew where he or she could find everyone because we always set up in the same places. Sandwiches were made the day before, and all one needed to do was walk up to the pavilion and request a sandwich, a Dixie cup (remember those?), soda, beer, sausages and peppers, and other tasty treats.

Watching the men play bocce was both entertaining and educational! When it came time for bocce, each man strolled into the woods and returned with two sticks. Tucking the sticks in their back pockets, the men began the game. Every time there was a close call as to whose ball was closest to the balleen, out came the sticks! Each man used his personal sticks to measure and was certain his measurement was the most accurate. It didn't surprise any of us that every game took hours to complete!

The pool was a unique experience! Fed by a nearby spring, it was usually bitter cold and contained whatever critters were lurking about in the spring at the time. We were kids, and neither the temperature nor the critters had any effect on us. We swam, dove, and played in that pool all day long, leaving long enough to walk up to the pavilion for more chow. Our moms told us we had to wait at least one hour per burger and a half-hour per hot dog, or we would get cramps and sink to the bottom. I don't recall ever finding one kid at the bottom of the pool at the end of the day.

There were also contests! From watermelon eating contests to pie eating contests, we took part in all of them. The big event was always the egg toss. Most of our parents were dressed in their Sunday best, something I still can't figure out, and competed in the egg toss, knowing that a bad throw or muffed catch would result in raw egg all over their clothing. Each time a round of tosses was completed, the lines were moved back a few feet. Eventually, they were throwing those things about twenty yards! It always amazed me how many of our parents

Bugsy cooling off at the Ladies Picnic.

could throw a raw egg that far, not to mention, catch it without wearing raw egg all over their body. Of course, the eggs did break, and one couple was left standing, heroes to us all!

At the end of the day, Rollie's dad and uncle drained the pool and gave all the kids a brush to scrub the sides and deck. We all did it, and we loved it! The entire time, the Russoli brothers sat on the bench and watched us clean their pool. It was always the best day of the summer!

Father's Day was another special time at the I-Club. Many of the men in the neighborhood were musicians, and they gathered in the street in front of the club with their instruments and await their conductor. Chester Frasetto led the band as they played marching music and many old Italian favorites. The balloon man worked the crowd, and by the end of the concert, every kid had a balloon tied to his or her wrist!

I remember walking down to the club with my dad and my sister, Anita to watch my mom bowl. There were men's and women's bowling leagues, and quite a few of the people from the neighborhood were on one team or another. Before the age of automatic pin-setters, the alleys were manned by the older boys from the neighborhood. My dad would take my sister and me to the kitchen for a steak sandwich and then we sat on the benches behind the bowlers. I still remember sitting on the rear bench in back of the pins with the "big guys" watching them set the pins. The bench was elevated to prevent anyone from being struck by a ball or stray pin, but some of the men could really fire a bowling ball! Once a pin flew up and hit the wall right next to the pin boy's head! They deserved whatever tips they received, if for no other reason than hazard pay!

My mom was a great bowler and won several trophies. I always enjoyed watching her bowl. I really loved those nights, especially because they were school nights, and we got to go to the club and hang out!

One summer, all the guys in our neighborhood got together and formed a league. We called it the "Teener League." We were all young, and we had a blast ending our day at the pool by heading to the I-Club to bowl. The girls with whom we hung out, came to the club loaded with cakes and cookies, and we would feast on these delicious treats as we bowled. At the end of our season, we used our dues to buy food and headed to Pine Tree Park for a bowling picnic. It was a great time and a fun way to end a summer day!

Waiting for the pasta!

Gathering by the Italian Club for a Father's Day concert.

13.

Downa Shore

Anyone living on the eastern side of Pennsylvania knows exactly what someone means when he says, "We're goin downa shore." Living in Allentown, just a short distance from Philadelphia, we were no exception. The "shore" referred to the Jersey Shore where places like Long Beach Island, Cape May, Avalon, Stone Harbor and Atlantic City provided families with a chance to get away from work and stress for a week or two to lie on the beach or body surf in the waves of the Atlantic Ocean. My family's choice for our vacation getaway was Wildwood, a town with wide beaches, plenty of restaurants, and a two-mile long boardwalk filled with food stands, games of chance, and enough rides to satisfy every kid.

Limited funds prevented our family and Tony's family from staying in a fancy hotel, but we could have cared less. We made the trip to Wildwood every summer with the Spagnoletti family and all ten of us spent the week in the first floor of the Three Sisters apartment building. Not surprisingly, the three sisters were Italian ladies and our parents enjoyed spending time with them as if they were family. They became family, since we made it a point to return to their place year after year. Our parents each had their own bedroom, and my sister Anita and Tony's sister Rosie shared the third bedroom. My brother was three or four years old at the time and stayed with my parents in their bedroom. That was the total number of bedrooms in the apartment, so Tony's brother, Louie, Tony, and I were relegated to the sofas. Louie, being the oldest, got his own sofa, while Tony and I shared the other. We spent the entire week sleeping on one sofa, my feet in Tony's face and Tony's feet up against my chin! It was imperative that we washed our feet thoroughly each night before bed!

We had about a three-block walk to the beach each morning, but we were so excited we didn't even mind the hike. Wildwood's beach, unlike some of the other New Jersey beaches, was amazingly long, stretching hundreds of yards before reaching the water. The boardwalk passed overhead as we continued our trek to the ocean.

Tony's dad was a shoe repairman and spent most of his time in the basement shop of the shoe store. Because of that, he really didn't get to spend much time in the sun. The first day on the beach, he lay on the blanket and fell asleep. No one wanted to disturb him, so he slept for hours. When it was time to head back to the apartment, he couldn't get up. Fried to a crisp and in total agony, he got to his feet with the help of my dad and mom and his wife. Dad walked back to the apartment and drove his car to the beach to pick him up. Lathered down with every skin cream known to mankind, he spent the next two days in the apartment before heading back to the beach where he covered himself with beach towels the rest of the week.

Tony and I spent the better part of everyday in the ocean, coming out long enough to eat lunch and then heading back into the waves. I remember my dad, wearing his United States Navy issue bathing cap as he floated on his back in the waves. Bathing caps were not uncommon for the women during those days. I don't remember seeing one girl or woman in the water without one of those rubber caps on her head. Pink, blue, yellow and white, some with rubber flowers on them, were all the rage. I could never understand why they wore them, but an even greater mystery to me was why my dad wore his. At least it was gun-metal gray and had the initials USN printed across the front. As much as I idolized my Dad and tried to emulate him in every way, I had no compunction to don one of those caps!

Dinner for ten in a very small kitchen was an adventure. As I said, money was tight, and a pot of boiling hot dogs or mounds of spaghetti was usually the meal du jour. One very special evening during the week, we went to one of the many restaurants in the town. That was a pretty special evening for us. I can probably count the number of times I had eaten at a restaurant on one hand and still had five fingers left over! It was fun, and I enjoyed it, but I don't think I realized how special that night was until years later. Like every kid, I probably complained about the food or having to share dessert with my sister, never realizing the sacrifice my parents made to take us out to a restaurant that evening. Thanks, Mom and Dad.

Early one morning, my sister and Rosie took my little brother with them for a stroll on the boardwalk. He was four years old at the time and required their utmost attention. Unfortunately, somewhere along the walk, they lost sight of him for a moment, and when they turned around, he was gone. I can't imagine what their three-block walk back to the house must have been like for them, knowing they had to tell my parents they lost my brother! It was early in the day, and we all dashed down to the beach and boardwalk to begin the frantic search for my brother. My parents checked with police officers on the boardwalk, while some of us talked to lifeguards and walked from blanket to blanket questioning every person on the beach. No luck.

The morning passed into afternoon with no sign of my baby brother. By this time, my Mom was a blubbering mess, thinking the worst. That afternoon, Dad and Mom and I got in the car and began driving up and down the streets of Wildwood. Windows down, we called his name and scanned the yards and houses but found nothing. When we returned to the apartment, Rosie's Mom, Dolly, informed my parents that they had left a call with the Wildwood Police Department, and the police had returned their call. They had my brother!

He had wandered off the boardwalk after slipping away from my sister and Rosie, strolled down the boardwalk entrance and walked two blocks into town where he joined in a birthday party on someone's lawn. The people who were throwing the party for their daughter assumed he was just one of the party-goers until the party ended and everyone was picked up by their parents. The owner of the house asked my brother who his parents were and when they were picking him up. He told him his mom's name is Irma and his dad's name is John. This mystified the man because neither he or his wife were familiar with either of these names. The man asked him where he lived, and he told him, "near my father's bakery." When the man pressed him about where this bakery was or the name of his bakery, he told the man, "My Dad's bakery is Roma." Searching the phonebook and finding no bakery in Wildwood by that name, the man called the police who promptly picked him up and took him back to the station. We celebrated that evening with more spaghetti and a birthday cake for my sister. I believe that it might have been, and most likely is, one of the best birthdays she has ever had.

Years later, our group of guys returned to Wildwood for a week's vacation. Our parents pulled some strings for us and got us the second floor of the Three Sisters apartment house. I was fifteen by that time, and only one of the three sisters was still alive and well.

Walking the boards one evening, my buddy Gerry and I stumbled upon a joke shop. We bought some goodies and returned to the apartment, stashing our bags under our bed. One of the guys in our group was really into the Italian thing and insisted we have breakfast at one of the Italian restaurants in town. He told us he would make a reservation and was very proud to let us know that he had "handled it." We heard about that reservation all day long the previous day as we relaxed on the beach and again that evening as we walked the boards. He was rather impressed with himself having made this important reservation at such a fine Italian restaurant.

Gerry and I decided this would be a perfect time to try out one of our "tricks" we had purchased at the joke shop. We chose a pouch filled with something called "foaming sugar" and tucked it away in Gerry's pocket before heading to the "famous" Italian restaurant. To this day, I'm not certain that an Italian restaurant is where I would choose to go for breakfast! Wouldn't something like "Joe's breakfast shop" make more sense? At any rate, we piled into my cousin's Packard and headed to Dom's Spaghetti House for breakfast. On the way to the restaurant, our friend let us know we didn't have to worry because he had made reservations! As we walked into a totally empty restaurant, our friend called out to no one in particular, "We have a reservation!" The tired-looking woman standing toward the rear of the restaurant looked at us and said, "Sit anywhere you want." So much for our reservation.

We sat at a table near the kitchen, hoping we would get faster service in the "crowded" restaurant that way, and while everyone was reading the menu, trying to find eggs and pancakes among the list of pasta, meatballs, and lasagna, Gerry slipped the pouch of foaming sugar from his pocket. Carefully, he opened the packet while I was removing the cap to the container of sugar. He quietly poured the "stuff" into the sugar container and screwed the cap back on without anyone noticing.

It was at that moment that our friend decided he wanted to sit near the window, and since there was no shortage of empty tables, we got up and moved, leaving the jar of foaming sugar behind. A few minutes later, an elderly couple (at least they were elderly to us) walked in and sat at the table at which we had originally been sitting. Apparently, they must have had a reservation too! I looked at Gerry, and we decided that it was unlikely that they were going to have coffee, and, if they did, they probably would take it black!

Our Italian breakfast of pancakes and bacon and eggs arrived, and we began to eat. I looked over to the other table in time to see the waitress set two coffees in front of the man and his wife. Oh boy! Gerry and I looked on in horror as the couple poured sugar into their cups. Instantly, their coffee began to erupt like Mt. St. Helens, spewing coffee all over the table! I could not believe how much coffee foamed from that damn cup! That stuff really worked! The owner was both flabbergasted and mystified, telling the couple that something like that never happened in his restaurant before. The guys at our table, except for Gerry and me, were also amazed at the sight, but we finished our breakfast and left the restaurant never to return to Dom's place again.

Walking the board walk one evening, we decided to enjoy one of the rides available at the amusement pier. The gentle coaster took us through mountains made of plaster and plywood cacti, traveling through tunnels and gold mines. Occasionally, an old prospector would pop his head up, and, with fire in his eyes, he fired his gun, telling everyone to stay clear of his claim! On one of the final turns at the top of the mountain, an Indian popped his head up from behind a rock. Chas chose this moment to reach out and push his head back down. Finishing the ride, we were greeted by three very large, very angry men. Before allowing us to leave the car, one of the men asked, "OK, which one of you pushed the Indian's head down?" We sat in silence with no intention of throwing Chas under the bus. We were escorted from the ride and told not to return. It wasn't that scary anyway!

When I was eighteen, Tony, Chas, Gerry and I decided it was time to hit a different shore town. We headed to Ocean City,

New Jersey - known for a younger crowd and a fun place to hang out. Not having a reservation (there's that word again), we drove around and found a motel with a vacancy sign. Unaware that the vacancy applied to the last available room, we checked in. In a fortunate stroke of serendipity, the entire motel, other than our room, was occupied by 200 girls from every high school sorority in Allentown, Pennsylvania. The mother lode!

The proprietor of the Shifting Sands Motel was named Alex. He seemed like a nice man who enjoyed feeding his rather large Doberman ice-cream cones. Alex watched over us like a strict father figure taking care of his children. The ratio of 200 girls to four guys was not lost on us as we sat by the pool surrounded by countless sorority girls walking around in two-piece bathing suits. Guys walking by the motel on their way to the beach stared in amazement, wondering how we managed to pull off such a major coup.

One afternoon as we sat by the pool with the girls, clouds rolled in, and it began to rain. As everyone scurried for cover, Tony nonchalantly lifted one of the umbrellas from its table stand and used it to walk to our room. Once there, he shook it out and leaned against the wall before entering our room. Within a minute, the door burst open, revealing a very angry Alex telling Tony to "Put that damn umbrella back where it belongs!" Later, when we saw Alex, he told us he was sorry for yelling like that because he really liked us.

Returning from the beach one day, we found many of the girls sitting on their suitcases on the sidewalk, all of them in tears. They told us that the maids complained to Alex about the sloppy condition of their rooms, and he told them they would have to leave. With no place to go, they just sat on the curb and cried.

"Not to worry," said Tony. "We'll talk to Alex." That was our Tony – coolest man on the planet! He said he would plead the girls case and make everything right. Amazingly, he did! Alex called all the girls together and paraded them past our open door to see how "four mature, young men" took care of their room. He then told them that if they promised to clean their rooms and model themselves after the boys, they could stay.

I'm certain that many of the girls gritted their teeth as they walked past our room, promising to "be more like them," but they were grateful to get their rooms back. We were treated like kings during the rest of the week.

14.

The Garbage Can

Allentown's elementary schools scattered throughout the city bore the names of United States presidents. Children learned their multiplication tables and ABC's in buildings named Washington, Lincoln, and Jefferson. Those of us in the Italian neighborhood attended the Garfield Elementary School named after our twentieth president, gunned down by an assassin six months after his election. Known affectionately as the "Garbage Can," it was the same school attended by many of our parents who were taught by many of the same teachers.

As was the case with the other neighborhood schools, the Garfield was located close enough to our homes to enable everyone to walk the few blocks to school.

None of the elementary schools had the luxury of a cafeteria. Because we were only a few blocks from our houses, we all went home for lunch. It was always cool when my mom was scheduled to work the counter at our luncheonette because on those days my friends and I went there for lunch. Instead of the traditional cheese sandwich and bowl of tomato soup, we dined on hot dogs, cheese steaks, and French fries and topped it all off with ice cream sundaes! This didn't happen often, but when it did, we certainly enjoyed ourselves!

Heading back to school for the afternoon session, we always stopped at Russoli's market for a supply of Nikl-Nip, small wax bottles containing some type of unknown liquid of various colors.

Lik em Aid was another delicacy. These were pouches of flavored sugar that one ate by licking one's finger and sticking it into the pouch before licking it off his hands. I'm not sure what was in that powdery substance, but it left our fingers discolored for a week. Another popular item were the small metal tins of paste sold with a one inch, crimped metal spoon. If one was not careful, he would slice his tongue at the very least or worst case scenario, swallow the spoon! The most amazing of the confections was the two-foot-long strip of paper with dots of sugar attached. When we plucked them off the strip, most of the paper stuck to the back of the sugar. I figured by the end of the week, I consumed an entire sheet of composition paper! Our final purchase before heading the three blocks to the Garfield was our assortment of wax lips and teeth!

As we waited outside for the bell signaling us to enter the building, entertainment was provided by the yo-yo man. Dressed in a tired-looking brown suit with frayed cuffs, he popped open the legs of his well-worn suitcase revealing a magnificent array of yo-yos. His wares, painted in a vast array of brilliant colors and studded with sparkling rhinestones, were an irresistible temptation to every boy and girl. He performed amazing feats with his yo-yos that dazzled us and emptied our pockets of the last of our change that we didn't spend at Russoli's.

In no time, we were "walking the dog" and "rocking the baby" with our coveted new toys. Unfortunately, the temptation to practice our tricks spilled over to the classroom, and our new yo-yos found their way into the desk drawer of our teacher. They remained there along with a countless number of cap guns, pea shooters, water pistols, and a vast array of wax lips and teeth for the remainder of the school year!

Halloween was observed by all the city elementary schools. Students returned to school after lunch dressed in costume. A favorite program on local television at the time featured a robot named Mister Rivets. Using cardboard, silver spray paint, wire, and old television tubes, my dad emerged from his workshop with my prize-winning costume. I was Mr. Rivets, the envy of every kid in the school! Each grade paraded through the neighborhood to the delight of our parents and other passersby before returning to school for a Halloween party that lasted until the end of the school day.

I volunteered to build a piñata for the party, knowing my dad would enjoy the challenge of building this special project. Together, we constructed a magnificent jack-o-lantern piñata, and I was awarded the honor of taking the first swing at the candy-filled pumpkin dangling from our classroom ceiling light fixture. Perhaps it was due to my little league baseball experience or just pure luck, but I gripped one of the flag poles used by the safety patrol and blasted that jack-o-lantern to smithereens with one swing! Unfortunately, my teacher had tied the blindfold so tightly over my eyes, by the time I was able to remove it, every piece of candy was gone! Not one lone tootsie roll or gum-ball remained on the classroom floor. As tears began to well in my eyes, my wise and benevolent teacher instructed each one of my classmates to deposit one piece of candy into my bag.

Because walking to school involved crossing several busy streets, parents entrusted the safety of their loved ones to the school safety patrol. The responsibility of serving on the safety patrol was bestowed upon members of the sixth-grade class. This, of course, was due in a large part to our advanced level of "maturity."

Members of the patrol were selected and voted upon by the sixth-grade class, and I was fortunate enough to be chosen along with eleven other lucky sixth graders. I will never forget putting on that white patrol belt across my chest. A silver badge was pinned on the belt signifying that we 'chosen few' represented law and order at our beloved "Garbage Can."

Two of our esteemed colleagues were issued special badges – a blue captain's badge was given to one of the boys, while a girl was presented with the red lieutenant's badge. Every member of the safety patrol had the utmost respect for our leaders; in fact, the captain and I were close friends. That said, every member of the safety patrol, myself included, envied him. We all dreamed of wearing the "blue badge"!

It was at the close of the school day when a snowball battle broke out on school property. In the interest of safety, the patrol was charged with the responsibility of making sure these snowball fights did not take place. The school day had officially ended at three o'clock, and I was returning from my assigned post three blocks from the school. Had I been guarding a street closer to the school, there is no doubt in my mind that I would have joined in the fray. I don't know any twelve-year old boy or girl who could resist a good, old-fashioned snowball battle. It's almost un-American!

It seemed like harmless fun to me, but our sixth-grade teacher, who hadn't yet left the building, saw it differently. Our captain was stripped of his position on the safety patrol, and in a special election, I was promoted to captain.

It may be argued that the honor was bestowed upon me by default, and only by the grace of the winter gods was I not present during the snowball fight. That said, I accepted my new rank and pinned the blue badge to my belt with great pride. A footnote to that story: The former captain and I remained close friends throughout that school year, junior high school, and high school graduation.

Three wires extended from the utility pole to the back of our house and crossed over our porch roof just outside my bedroom window. The bottom wire was six inches above the porch roof with the other two wires spaced evenly six inches apart. After an evening snow fall, I eagerly looked out my window at the three wires. If the snow was below or level with the bottom wire, I knew I hadn't a snowball's chance (pun intended) of missing school that day. In today's litigious society when children ride buses to school and wait at bus stops near busy roads, even the slightest suggestion of a slippery road keeps students home in front of their TV's and video games.

The snow had to reach at least the second or third wire before any school in our neighborhood did the unthinkable and closed for the day! Every so often we were lucky enough to experience one of those "two or three wire" days.

After wolfing down our breakfast, my sister and I donned our leggings, wrapped Holsum bread bags over our three layers of socks, struggled into our snow boots and headed to Fifth and Cedar Street. Ironically, standing on the corner of those two streets was the very school that was closed to spare the children from having to walk there in the snow!

Beginning on Cedar Street, Fifth Street was a steep drop, passing over three cross streets before ending at the railroad tracks which passed in front of Jordan Park. Crossing the three intersections was not a problem for sledders since the Allentown Police Department erected traffic barricades at each intersection, closing the streets to motorists. Occasionally, a driver chose to move the barricade, leaving sledders to swerve and dodge the passing automobile!

Two hour delays were not part of our school day. It was "all or nothing," opened or closed. One morning a blanket of fine, freezing rain coated the streets and sidewalks of the neighborhood. Without any possibility of a delay, my sister, who is a few years older than I and much wiser to the ways of the world, said to me, "Fall down." I was somewhat confused until she whispered to me, "Mom is watching us from the porch, fall down!" I did my very best Jerry Lewis pratfall and went flying. My sister, in a performance worthy of an Oscar, attempted to help me up only to fall on top of me. Mom immediately called to us saying that no children of hers were going to injure themselves trying to get to school! My sister, if nothing else, was wise....and quite devious!

City snow plows rarely found their way into our neighborhood. If there was a heavy snowfall, everyone on our street took part in the cleanup. Because none of the houses had a driveway, parking was limited to the space in front of our houses. Once a space was cleared by any of the families, it was an unwritten law that said space belonged to that family. Ownership of one's space was demonstrated by various pieces of furniture strategically placed to prevent interlopers from taking advantage of an open parking space. Kitchen chairs, end tables, and coffee tables were on display throughout the neighborhood. It was a comical sight to see everyone's living room perched out in the street!

It had been snowing hard one night when my mom returned from her waitressing job. After moving our furniture out of the way, Mom proceeded to park her car. In her defense, there was no street light in front of our house, and the snow was rather intense. To help negotiate her parking space, she turned down her car window to see how close she was to the curb. Having successfully parked her car, Mom locked the doors and went into the house for a well-deserved night of sleep.

My dad, whose day at the bakery began at 4 AM, went outside to shovel Mom's car out before heading to work. Mom had parked the car perfectly. Unfortunately, she forgot to roll the windows closed. Before my dad could clear Mom's space, he had to shovel the inside of the car which was filled with snow from the seats to the ceiling! The following evening while Mom was at work, someone from the silk mill had moved the furniture and parked in our sacred space in front of the house. My dad was unhappy but resolute. Dressed in his winter clothes, he went out front with his shovel and proceeded to bury the mill worker's car in a mountain of snow! The silk mill's second shift ended a few hours before my mom was to arrive home from the restaurant, and the parking culprit trudged to his car after an eight-hour shift to find his car buried with snow. Feeling sorry for the man, who had just worked a full shift and was standing in front of his car without any means to clear the snow, Dad suited up, went outside, and cleared the snow from his car. The man was forever grateful and never knew that it was my dad who buried his car in the first place. That was the kind of man my dad was. He had made his point, but he would not let that poor man struggle to get his car out after a hard day's work.

As the chill of a Pennsylvania winter gave way to spring, Garfield, as well as the other elementary schools, participated in the annual ritual known as May Day. With our parents seated on folding chairs set up on the playground, the festivities began with the procession of the queen and her court. One special sixth-grade girl followed her court to her position of honor as music blared through the PA system. With the May Queen looking on from her throne and our parents, armed with their eight- millimeter movie cameras watching, each grade performed a dance on the large circle painted in the center of the playground. Every class's dance was choreographed by the school district's musical director, a no-nonsense task-master who was all business and settled for nothing less than absolute perfection.

The day culminated with the dance of the May-pole. As the sixth-grade class danced around the May-pole, weaving their crepe streamers over and under each other, the pole with its flowered top rose higher and higher. The rite of spring was accomplished once again!

An annual ice-cream festival put a final punctuation point on the school year, and we walked home, having completed our first school adventure. Junior high school was next, and we couldn't wait to begin this new adventure of our lives.

Left: Mom and I looking out for the bad guys.

Right: Mom's little girl.

15.

BoBo and the F Word

For over one hundred years, the fairgrounds at Seventeenth and Liberty has been the site of the Great Allentown Fair. During our time in elementary school, the fair took place in September. since the school year had already begun, students were dismissed at 11:30 to allow children to attend the fair.

The two midways at the fair featured something for all age groups. There were rides for everyone, including a double Ferris wheel which lit up the night sky and could be seen for several blocks before we neared the entrance gates. Games of chance stood alongside food concessions offering pierogis and funnel cakes as well as local favorites from Yocco's hot dogs and Vince's steak sandwiches.

Fair goers put their quarters down on numbers at the candy wheel, hoping to win boxes of Snickers or Clark bars, while others bought large sheets covered with numbers from the blanket man. Several of the blankets in our house were won by my mom at the blanket man's stand. Kids walked through the midway carrying small bowls of goldfish. The kids won these by tossing a ping pong ball into the bowl. I never could understand what they did with those bowls when they went on the rides, and I suspect that most of the fish never lived to see the next day.

Young men showed off their athletic skills to their girlfriends by slamming a large mallet onto a spring board attempting to ring a bell at the top or by shooting basketballs into very small hoops to win that elusive stuffed animal for their sweetie. Tony and I enjoyed playing the game where one needed to shoot a water pistol into a clown's mouth. The water triggered a device that inflated a balloon on his head. When someone burst the balloon on the clown's head, that patron won a prize. The clown's head was moving back and forth at the time, making it difficult to keep a steady aim. There were eight pistols and we were always competing against six other patrons. When the bell sounded and the clown heads began to move, Tony and I focused on one clown mouth. With double the water going into our clown, we were a cinch to win almost every time! The person operating the stand never saw what we were doing because he was watching the balloons on the clown heads. Yes, we cheated! I'm not proud to say it, but somebody's balloon was going to burst first, so it might as well be ours!

Sideshows such as Eeka, the snake lady, and the mighty Atom were other popular attractions. The Atom was an aging strongman with a long beard who bent nails and horse shoes. Eeka sat in a cage with a bunch of snakes slithering over her legs while she nibbled on something resembling a snake skin. The favorite side show on the midway was Bobo, the clown. Bobo would tease, insult, and cajole fair goers into spending dollar after dollar to throw baseballs at a small target attempting to drop Bobo into a tank of water. Having spent most of their food money to teach Bobo a lesson and pay him back for his insults, these fair goers walked smugly away feeling like they had "shown Bobo who was boss" while Bobo, who had just enjoyed a cool dunk on a rather hot day, smiled and counted his money!

When I was twelve years old, my friends and I spent much of our time hanging out at the many basketball courts throughout the neighborhood. These "courts" were nothing more than backboards and rims fastened to any convenient utility pole. As we waited for the older boys to finish their game, I learned the "words of the street" for the first time, including the oft used "F" word, spoken at least a dozen times during every pick-up game of basketball! Tony and I were enjoying an afternoon at the fair with our moms and had just boarded the Round-up, a stomach churning ride that could have been used to train astronauts!

In the meantime, our moms strolled across the midway to the bingo tent for a game or two of bingo. When the harrowing Round-up settled to a full stop, Tony and I disembarked and walked on rubbery legs to the midway looking for our mothers. Searching everywhere through the crowded midway, we began to panic. Suddenly, my mom and Tony's mom appeared on the other side of the midway. It was then that I shouted the words that would forever live in infamy and forever strip away my innocence. At the top of my lungs, I yelled to my mom, "Where the F--- were you?"

My mom was young at the time, and years of bowling and waitressing strengthened her legs. That said, I never saw that woman close the ground between her and me with such breakneck speed! With fire in her eyes, she grabbed my shoulders and began shaking me, demanding to know where I learned such a word. Tony's mom caught up to us just in time to hear me say, "I learned it from Tony!" Yes, I threw my best friend under the bus that day. Tony's eyes bugged out of his head as his mom began to throttle him and I could only look on in despair, my eyes pleading for forgiveness. Years later, I thought back on that betrayal, I thought that perhaps it was pay back for Tony having told me to sing "Shrimp Boats" in front of Gerry. It doesn't matter because Tony was cool with what happened that day, and we both survived.

When I was fourteen years old, my mom and I had another chance encounter on the midway of the Great Allentown Fair. In the early sixties, the fair featured several burlesque shows. Our group of guys gathered at doc's drugstore preparing for a night at the fair. Before we left, we bought a bunch of cigars. I am a life-long non-smoker, but that night was a special occasion.

After a stroll through the midway, we lit our cigars and headed to a strip show in one of the burlesque tents. The seven of us sat in our seats puffing on our cigars waiting for the show to begin when our moms walked into the tent. I'm not sure if one can swallow an entire lit cigar; however, I think I came as close as humanly possible ! To their credit, our moms looked at us, smiled and turned back towards the stage. I always wondered if our moms were as alarmed by our seeing them as we were at their seeing us!

The following morning, I braced myself for the onslaught of my father's wrath, but it never came. It was one of those small miracles a boy never questions.

Years later, I became an employee at the Allentown Fair. My neighbor asked me if I could use a little extra money during fair week, and I was glad to take her up on it. I hired on at Big-hearted Benny's Bingo Stand for two dollars an hour, and I feel as if I earned every penny of my salary. The first day on the job, we were told to set up the bingo tent. I had a Pecos Bill tent in which my friends and I used to sleep on warm, summer evenings in my back yard. This was not such a tent! A huge tractor-trailer delivered the tent, and it took every worker to haul it to the site. It was propped up with twenty-four, eight-inch by eight-inch posts, which required us to drive dozens of large steel spikes into the fair ground's asphalt to secure it in place. Once that was accomplished, we had to erect the center shelving used to hold the myriad of prizes. The next step was to put together the long tables and stools needed for the bingo patrons. Finally, one person was told (never asked) to crawl under the flashing and connect the electric cables. Guess who was fortunate enough to get that job?

We began working on the tent at seven in the morning on a very hot August day. At noon, one of the guys asked "Big Hearted" Benny if we could take a lunch break. Benny fired him on the spot.

The tent flaps were held up by long steel bars running through the inside of the flap, and while we were putting up the tent, I noticed that we were too close to a utility pole to allow the flap on that side of the tent to be put in place without bumping into the pole. I took it upon myself to walk over to Benny and point out this problem, suggesting that perhaps we should move the tent about seven feet away from the pole. Benny went ballistic! How dare I suggest to a man who has been putting his tent up in fairgrounds all over the Eastern Seaboard how to do his job! I was told to get back to work and thank the stars I wasn't fired.

After many hours, the tent was erected, and some of the workers were directed to put the flaps up. Of course, I already knew that the flap on the one side of the tent wasn't going to work, and I waited for Benny to apologize to me. Instead, when the flap failed to lock into place, Benny charged over to me, calling me, among other things, a "stupid kid" who should know better. I quit on the spot and left the site. My brother, who was also working the job, came after me and talked me out of quitting. He told me to just let it go, that Benny was just being Benny. I agreed to come back, and never once did "Big Hearted" Benny ever apologize.

Since we needed seven more feet for the flap to be put up (the distance I suggested to Benny before we put up the tent) Benny told us we would have to "move the joint!" That may sound simple enough, but moving a tent with twenty-four eight-by-eight posts meant moving each post a few inches at a time until all twenty-four posts, along with a ton of canvas, were moved seven feet!

Benny instructed us to lift each post off the ground, move it two or three inches and then move on to the next post. Watching this excruciatingly slow process for about ten minutes, I grabbed one of the sledge hammers used to drive in the tent stakes and began knocking each post over about three inches before moving on to the next one. I was making great progress until Benny came out of his air-conditioned trailer and saw what I was doing. Once again, he ripped into me, saying I was ruining the posts, so it was back to the "lifting" method. About twenty minutes later, one of the guys went back to using the sledge hammer. Noting how much faster this method was working, Benny told all of us to "get a sledge hammer and do what he's doing!"

When the tent was successfully moved the seven feet, Benny praised the young man for his ingenuity and suggested that we could all learn something from him. My brother looked at me as if to say, "Let it go," and I did. We had been there over thirteen hours before the tent and the interior stands were completed. Bone-weary and hungry, we began walking to our cars when Benny's wife called to tell him she had been in a traffic accident and needed someone to drive to the scene and pick her up. I wasn't fast enough, and before I could get through the fairground gate, Benny called me back and told me to pick up his wife. I was to drive his Cadillac, but he would go along. I wanted to ask if he was going along in his car and what he needed me for, but I didn't.

We arrived just as the tow truck finished hooking up her car, and she got into the rear of Benny's Cadillac. All I wanted to do at that point was to get them back to the fairgrounds, park his car, and drive my car home. However, before that could happen, Benny told me that we needed to follow the tow truck to the garage. I told him there was no reason to do that. They knew what they were doing and would contact him after they got his wife's car safely secured. Benny said to me, "You can't trust these people." " Sometimes they drop the car off the truck." I assured him that something like that never happened, but he insisted we follow the truck.

Sure enough, a few blocks from the garage, the truck dropped her car! I'm not making this up, they dropped her car! I had to wait until they reconnected the car and for Benny to inspect the car for further damage before driving the rest of the way to the garage. After returning Benny and the Mrs. back to the fairgrounds, I drove home. By that time, it was about nine o'clock, and Benny reminded me that he expected me by seven a.m. "Big Hearted"!

We worked the bingo stand from nine a.m. until two a.m. for the ten-day run of the fair, and on the final day of the run, we had to tear down the tent and interior stands and load them on the truck. We closed the bingo stand at two a.m. and began the tear down. We were nearing the end of the work around eight o'clock the following morning when I stepped on a nail, driving it through my sneaker and into my foot. The emergency room of the Allentown Hospital was directly across the street from the fairgrounds, and one of the guys asked Benny if he could drive me over. Benny said, "No, it's not that far, he can hop over." Benny called me into his trailer and told me that I was a nice guy, but since I hurt my foot, he couldn't use me anymore and fired me. I spent many years after that attending the fair, and every time I walked past that tent with the large red heart across the front, I smiled. "Big Hearted"!

The grandstand at the Great Allentown Fair featured hundreds of big-time performers over the years. Stars such as Andy Williams and The Supremes were just a few of the attractions in the 1960's. The '70s showcased Johnny Cash, Johnny Carson, Liza Minelli and a host of others, while Pat Benatar and Rod Stewart were among the stars who rocked the '80s. One of the big names to perform at the fair in the '60's was a guy by the name of Liberace. Yes, the great Liberace graced the grandstand stage of the Allentown Fair to a sold-out crowd!

Mom was waitressing at Anna Maria's Italian Restaurant at the time when Liberace and his entourage came in for dinner between his performances. After dinner, he chatted with my mom, telling her he wished he could go to some quiet place and relax before heading back to the fair. Mom suggested our house. Dad and I were watching "The Untouchables" on TV when we heard footsteps on the stairs, and there was Liberace standing in our basement! He asked Dad if he could join us and sat down to watch TV. I was dumbfounded, but my dad never broke stride. He continued to watch TV like there was nothing out of the ordinary going on in our house.

Dad was a smoker at the time, and Liberace turned to him and asked for a cigarette. Dad smiled and said, "Don't you even have your own cigarettes?" "You have to mooch from me?" Silence was followed by laughter, and Dad shared his smokes with him like they were old friends. Just another night watching TV with my dad and Liberace!

16.

Swan Song

During the 1950s, accordion academies began to spring up all over the valley. Dick Contino was popular at the time, in fact, my dad had several of his albums. Every boy and girl longed to pick up a "squeeze box" and play a few choruses of "Lady of Spain" complete with a healthy bellows shake. Anyone who has grown up in the '50s and has taken accordion lessons knows what a bellows shake is! Like so many aspiring musicians, I begged my mom and dad to sign me up for lessons. I began my musical career at Keyboard Studios on Ridge Avenue in Allentown. Beginning with a twelve bass, mini accordion, I sat in a tiny studio with my first instructor. I was on my way! My first selection was called "Batter Up," a lesson in learning the scales disguised as a song.

Each week Dad drove me to Keyboard for my half-hour lesson. At the end of the lesson, students were rewarded, or not rewarded, depending on how well the lesson went, with "music bucks." These green bills were worth one hundred dollars each, and had a picture of an accordion in the center of the bill. A typical lesson garnered the student two of the bills. If the lesson was outstanding, one could expect a bump to three bills. To my credit, I had some three hundred dollar lessons, but to be honest, I also pulled down only one hundred on some days, and I can even recall walking out with no money! Hey, everybody has a bad day.

Students used these bills to purchase items from the glass showcase in the front of the studio. I thought it was a pretty good deal until I checked the price of a baseball glove and discovered it cost $15,000. I was young and naive, but smart enough to see through that little scheme. Sure, the reward for a lesson well-done encouraged students to practice. It could serve as a great motivator, but even if the kid became disenchanted with the instrument and wanted to quit, he wanted that glove badly enough to keep going for lessons, and Mom and Pop footed the bill!

Every parent wants to see some sort of payoff for their hard-earned dollars. Thus, the recitals and, more importantly, the contests! I entered my first contest in the concert room of the studio and played the "Village Tavern Polka." Everyone in the contest was good, but when the applause meter, yes, they really used an applause meter, was finished tallying the decibel levels, I had won the ultimate prize: a plastic trophy with a genuine gold-painted accordion on top! I would have preferred the baseball glove.

I continued with lessons for several years and became prolific with that squeeze box. I was scheduled to perform in an accordion contest in Willow Grove Amusement Park in Philadelphia. It had been raining for several days, and the day we were getting ready to drive to Philadelphia, the rain was falling in torrents. I really wasn't a big fan of performing in front of a crowd, and this was a regional contest, in Philly, no less! It became obvious to me that there was no way the contest would not be postponed, and, even if it weren't, there was no way my Dad was going to risk his entire family, not to mention his beloved Ford Customliner in that kind of weather. I was wrong. The show was on, and we were going. I put on my coat and tie and joined my family in our trusty Ford to brave the storm in the name of musical history!

The contest was held in an outdoor band-shell which, fortunately, had a roof over the stage as well as the audience. When it was my turn to perform, I looked out over the crowd, and for one moment, I could have sworn I saw a huge, white swan passing by the rear of the band-shell! As I played, I saw more of these swans and realized that these were the park's sight-seeing boats, carried away from their little pond in the park by rising flood waters and now heading toward the highway like some menacing-looking creatures from another planet! I know I won something, but I don't remember if it was a first -place trophy, or an award for being the bravest (or dumbest) kid willing to leave Allentown in the middle of a flood. And it was a flood! As soon as the contest ended, every parent and kid bolted to their car, hoping to escape Philadelphia with their lives! The water was still rising, and the swans were now drifting out of the park and across the highway into a supermarket parking lot. It was a surreal sight, and would have been quite amusing if everyone weren't totally frightened out of their wits! As we passed the supermarket, we saw swans the size of school buses banging into the storefront of the market. I can only imagine what the people inside the store must have thought as they gazed at these monsters trying to invade the check-out lines!

The only things visible in the parking lot were the antennas of the automobiles as we passed by in our, hopefully, trusty Customliner! Dad remained calm, and that's the only reason the rest of us didn't panic, but I knew we were all scared to death! Somehow, we made it to Allentown. Our 1952 Ford performed like the true champion it was! The following day, we learned on the news that several people had been washed from the automobiles and drowned.

We enjoyed many outdoor gatherings during the summer, some at parks and others in the back yards of neighbors and family. My friends and I always had great times, enjoying a game of catch, playing lawn games, even swimming in someone's pool. These were perfect afternoons with good friends that always seemed to come to a screeching halt when I saw my mom setting up my music stand in the yard and Dad lugging my accordion out of our trunk. The next thing I knew, folding chairs were being set up, including one by my music stand, and for me, the fun was over! Our older Italian friends sat down and readied themselves for my version of "Oh Marie." I played, they sang, while my friends continued to play touch football. I knew my accordion days were numbered. One night, I broke the solemn news to Mom and Dad. I was finished with the accordion. I told them I had lost interest and wanted them to save their money and stop paying for lessons. It was a noble gesture on my part, thinking only of them and the need to save them money! My accordion, hand -made in Italy, was stowed in the closet with the understanding that it was there for me whenever I changed my mind. There were occasions when I brought that squeeze box out, one of which I will mention in the next chapter of this book, but for all purposes, the accordion stage of my life was over.

17.

Christmas in the Hood

Christmas is a very special time of year in everyone's life, and it was no different for those of us living in the Italian section of Allentown. I always enjoyed working in Dad's bakery and having the opportunity to talk with our neighbors when they stopped by for bread or just to visit. During the holidays, they stopped by not only to pick up their bread for the day but also to deliver a little gift to us. It may have been a bottle of homemade wine, a fresh salami, also homemade, or perhaps a panettone, a freshly-baked Italian coffee cake. We could always rely on Dewey to stop by with a few of his hand-made silk ties during one of his visits to the shop during the holidays.

We set up my sister's reel to reel tape recorder on top of one of the dough machines and played Christmas music during the day while we worked and even sang along with some of the songs as we worked. After we closed the bakery for the day, Dad and I walked back to the house for lunch before returning to the shop. Dad would use our small mixer to whip up several pounds of sugar cookie dough, and I'd call the guys to let them know we were ready to bake. With the tape recorder piping out its Christmas music, we spent the afternoon making cookies. Tony and I, along with Gerry, Chas and Rollie rolled dough, cut out cookies, and decorated them. There was a smaller gas oven in the shop, so we didn't have to fire up the hearth oven with coal to bake the cookies.

Gerry's brother had been injured in an automobile accident

and was confined to a wheelchair. We wanted to include him in most everything we could, so we brought him to the bakery to help us out. Tony decided to do a little "free-handed" cookie cutting, and using a knife, cut out a wheelchair and decorated it to look like Bobby's chair. Bobby loved it! It was a special afternoon, but it was a special time of year, and every one of the people in that bakery was a special person!

Dad went all out at Christmas time, setting up an elaborate Christmas display in our basement. After moving all the furniture from one end of the room, Dad and I set up two large platforms spaced two feet apart. One of the platforms was a display of a city, complete with streets, a park, houses and an airport. Using a small motor and a wire, Dad had an airplane flying over the terminal, and the streets were crowded with people and automobiles. The city contained a hospital, police station as well as a fire station, a school, and countless numbers of grocery stores, diners, and restaurants.

The other platform was a complete rural setting with farm houses, pastures, and barns. A corral contained a myriad of cows, horses, and sheep as well as chickens. Located on the country-side of the display was a dairy platform on which a "refrigerated" milk car would stop and unload miniature cans of milk.

An extensive network of track enabled the four trains to travel from one platform to another, crossing over the space between them by way of two steel bridges. An enormous mountain, constructed by my dad out of wood, screen, and several pounds of plaster sat in one corner of the display. One of the trains passed through the mountain while another used a set of trestles to make its way onto the mountain on its journey to the other side. Using several large paper flour bags fastened together, Dad painted over twenty-five feet of scenery which he and I attached to the walls behind the two platforms. A few hundred feet of wires ran beneath the platforms and connected to an elaborate control center which included light switches, track switches, and several transformers needed to operate the engines of the four trains. It was an amazing display, and everyone in the neighborhood came by every year to marvel at its beauty.

Not satisfied with just having the inside display, Dad decorated the front porch of our row house with more than Christmas lights. He built two huge bells out of chicken wire and covered them with foil. Using the motor from my erector set, he set these bells in motion allowing them to swing back and forth in perfect synchronization. Next, using one of my sister's old dolls, he installed moving parts inside the head and arms, built an organ complete with pipes, and seated the doll in front of the keyboard. Mom was the seamstress in our family and dressed the doll to look like an angel. When Dad threw the switch, the angel's arms reached down and appeared to be playing the organ, while her head moved side to side.

He needed one more part to make his display perfect. Hiding a speaker on the porch, its wires leading into his workshop, Dad attached them to his stereo. There was no such thing as wireless anything in those days! Dad turned on all the switches, put a Christmas album of organ and bell music (who has something like that?) and the display came alive. With the bells swaying and the angel tapping the painted keys of the organ, music brought the entire scene to life! Passing cars stopped, and drivers rolled their windows down to listen and watch.

Interestingly, with all of Dad's Christmas spirit, he succumbed to one of the tackier trends of the 1960's. After setting up the most beautiful Christmas trees and decorating them with glass ornaments, colorful lights and loads of tinsel, Dad stunned us all one Christmas by replacing our traditional tree with an aluminum one! He purchased a revolving color wheel to illuminate this monstrosity in shades of blue, green, red, and orange. We were shocked! My sister and I loved our dad, and we were so proud of his porch display and Christmas platform, but we hated that tree!

One night a few days before Christmas, Sis and I drove to a Christmas tree lot in search of a real tree only to find the lot to be virtually empty. In a scene from Charlie Brown's Christmas, we found a sad-looking, scrawny tree and decided it was better than the "aluminum tree from hell." The tree lost half its needles during the drive home and had large, empty spaces on one of its sides, but we were determined to replace Dad's tree. After confronting Dad and sharing our true feelings about his tree, Dad relented and agreed to replace his tree with ours. He went to his workshop, returned with his electric drill, and proceeded to drill holes in the trunk of our tree. He then cut some branches from the other side of the tree and stuck them into the holes he had drilled. When he finished, we had to admit, it looked "almost normal." The tree didn't last too long, but it didn't have to, since it was only a few days before Christmas. We never saw the aluminum tree again!

One of our group's favorite things to do during the Christmas season was to pile in the car and drive through the neighborhood, looking at everyone's Christmas displays. We gathered at Tony's house where Tony's sister Rosie was busy painting her traditional Christmas scenes on two floor to ceiling mirrors in their living room. Every year was a new scene, and she did a beautiful job with her artwork. We'd sit for a while in Tony's house as Johnny Mathis sang "The Christmas Song" on the stereo, before heading out to view the lights.

Bordering Allentown to the east, was the city of Bethlehem, PA. Not surprisingly, Bethlehem was known as the Christmas City, and every shop and home was aglow with Christmas lights while carolers stood on street corners singing their favorite songs. In the center of the Hill to Hill Bridge stood a thirty-foot tree covered with thousands of lights. The highlight of Bethlehem at Christmas time was the Christmas star that stood on a mountain top. At night, when the mountain was shrouded in darkness, the star appeared to be shining in the sky. After we had driven through the Bethlehem streets, we drove to the top of the mountain to the star. It looks so small from the city below, but is in fact ninety-one feet tall and forty feet wide. It was originally a wooden structure but was eventually converted to steel girders from, where else, Bethlehem Steel.

One Christmas Eve we gathered at Tony's house, which was always filled with festive, Christmas cheer. We toasted with a little holiday cheer in front of Rosie's beautiful mirrors before setting out in the neighborhood for some Christmas caroling. Our band, The Gentrys, was still together at the time, so we had some music to accompany our singers (I'll have more to say about the Gentrys later in this story). Since I couldn't carry my keyboard around the neighborhood, I used my accordion instead. Yes, that very same accordion that my dad had put away in the closet many years earlier was resurrected from its dark storage to make music one more time! Tony, the Gentrys' drummer, brought one of his drums along, while Tony's cousin, Chuck, our sax player, provided a little woodwind sound to the festivities. Our other band members weren't part of the neighborhood and were celebrating Christmas with their families, so the musical accompaniment was limited to the three of us.

We strolled through the streets of our neighborhood, stopping at our neighbors' homes to sing carols, and occasionally, we were asked inside to join the family in a little "Christmas cheer." Charlie Russoli was the Allentown City Treasurer at the time and always had a festive Christmas Eve bash going on in his home. He welcomed the entire group into his home, and we enjoyed several glasses of champagne before continuing our journey. My accordion began to grow heavier as the evening wore on, and seemed to cause me to become a bit "wobbly" also.

At the end of the evening, my dear friends put me in Tony's car with my accordion and drove to downtown Allentown. We had a friend who lived in an apartment in the city. I'm not sure of her name, but we had nick-named her Moose. The guys carried me upstairs and deposited me on her bed, setting my accordion on top of my chest and left me there with a very irate, young lady! When I awoke on Christmas morning, it took me awhile to figure out that I was not in Kansas, nor was I in my house getting ready for Christmas Mass! Moose was no less thrilled at my being there than I was, and I used her phone to call Tony. After Tony was through laughing, I told him to get his fanny to Moose's apartment and pick me up before my mom and dad found out I wasn't in my room dressing for church.

Trooper that he was, and to this day, still my best friend, Tony headed to Moose's place and drove me and my hand-made-in Italy accordion home. As I opened the front door, I was greeted by my sister, who told me to get my butt upstairs and get ready for church before Mom and Dad came down for breakfast!

After attending mass at Our Lady of Mr. Carmel on Christmas morning, everyone in the neighborhood took part in the traditional Christmas event of "making the rounds." Because ours was such a tight-knit neighborhood, and everyone lived so close together, it was easy to walk from one house to another, passing each other on the street as we strolled by. Our houses were open to all that ventured to stop by, and everyone was welcome to stop in for a box of Italian nougat candy, some cookies, and a shot of brandy. We weren't old enough to drink and didn't make a practice of it, but our parents and neighbors knew it was a special morning, and we weren't going to be getting in a car, so one shot of apricot brandy was acceptable.

Eventually, we would get to my house, which was usually already crowded with the "older" groups of guys and gals who were enjoying some Christmas cheer along with Dad's delicious baked goods. In addition to his wonderful cookies, Dad, whose mother was of Hungarian descent, also made kiffles and the best strudel on the planet! The guys always wanted to get their hands on the control panel of Dad's platform, and despite his admonition to "keep away from the controls," they knew he was too busy entertaining our friends and neighbors to pay any attention to them. They threw the switches on the control panel and started the trains flying around the tracks. Before I could get them to slow the trains down, they crashed one of them inside the mountain! The guys purposely did this every year, and Dad would have to get out his pole with the hook at one end to drag the train out of the mountain. He built that pole for that very reason, knowing it was a Christmas tradition of my friends to crash the train inside the mountain.

Whenever we learned that the Christmas Mass held in the morning was a "High Mass" we chose to go to Mass on Christmas Eve instead. A High Mass was a bit more involved and lasted about a half hour longer than a regular Mass, so we opted for the Midnight Mass. Most people, including my parents, also preferred to do the same.

Our group of guys arrived at the church in Ritchie's car about five minute before midnight. The Italian church was not very large, and the likelihood of finding a seat inside was very remote by that time. Not wanting to miss Mass, we stood in the stairwell of the church. We could see and hear everything from our position on the stairs, so it wasn't a problem. During the service, a man walked into the front door of the church and whispered to us that he was parked in by the cars in the street. He had been unfortunate enough to arrive at his destination early enough to find a parking space on the street and was just a few cars away from the front of our church. It was not uncommon for the congregation to double park in front of the church during services. After all, it couldn't possibly be illegal to park that way if one was on his way to church! The man explained to us that he had been visiting his daughter and was now ready to return home. All of this was taking place while the Mass was going on at the top of the stairs.

After some deliberation, Tony told him it would be OK if he drove his car onto the sidewalk and along the walk until he arrived at the end of the street. He could then drive off the curb and be on his way. I know Tony, and he has a heart of gold. He wanted to help this man, and he felt this was the only way he would be able to get his car out of there. The gentleman considered Tony's suggestion and proceeded to get in his car and pull it up onto the sidewalk. It was working, and he looked like a cinch to make it to the end of the sidewalk. As he approached the front door of our church, he swerved to his right to avoid the utility pole in front of the church and his car became lodged between the pole and the front door of our church. While we stood there trying to figure out what to do next, Mass ended and the front door to the church opened about a foot before wedging itself against the man's car door. The congregation began to squeeze out the front door while the man remained imprisoned in his car with all of us standing there looking on. The less-than-happy worshippers continued to squeeze through the front door, and I knew it was only a matter of time before my mom and dad came through that portal!

The look on my dad's face as he worked his way through the door let me know I was in for another long night when I got home. We all got together and pushed the man's car as he drove, and it finally broke free. As he drove off, his car dented on both sides, he rolled down his window, said "Thank you" and wished us a Merry Christmas. In no great hurry to return home that night, knowing our parents were less than thrilled with us, we went to the Jordan Bowling Alley, which was open 24 hours even on Christmas Eve! We bowled until three o'clock in the morning and headed home. In the morning, we were awakened by the news that the Jordan Bowling Alley had burned to the ground during the "early morning hours" of Christmas! I'm not sure if there's a message in there somewhere, but it left us to wonder. By the way, we did nothing but bowl that night, and the building was fine when we left.

18.

Three Balls for a Quarter

Before the Allentown Italian Club contained an asphalt parking lot complete with lined spaces in the rear of the building, the space was nothing more than hard clay and an empty field. To add money to the coffers of the club treasury, a traveling carnival was brought in once a week every summer. The lot was a short walk from our home, and walking through the alley behind our house, we could get to the lot in less than two minutes. To young kids, this was a dream come true! A carnival with rides and games and plenty of food two minutes from our door!

After a day of swimming and immediately upon finishing dinner, we headed to the lot to watch the men setting up the rides and stands that were to house various games of chance and food. We had all attended carnivals in other places, and the Allentown Fair provided much more entertainment, but the one thing we had never done was work at one of these places. As we watched the carnival slowly come together, it was easy to tell who the people in charge were, and they were the ones we needed to impress! We stood by the bosses as they barked out instructions to their workers and did our best to show interest in what they were doing.

Asking questions without becoming too overbearing, we gained their respect and admiration. I never hesitated to point out to these men that my dad's bakery was right next to the lot, and I had spent many summers working in the shop. I was a good worker, just ask my dad. As the day neared for the grand opening, one of the bosses came over to Tony and me and asked if we would like a job. Not wanting to appear too anxious, we told him we might be interested since we were not busy that week. How cool were we?

We were hired to run one of the games of chance and given a ten-minute tutorial on the game. It was a stand containing two sections of barrels, cut in half and turned upside down. On each barrel sat three bottles made of lead. The bottles were stacked, with two of them sitting on the barrel, and the third bottle balanced on the top of the two lower bottles. Twenty feet away was a wooden counter stacked with baseballs in piles of three. A canvas drop-cloth hung behind the barrels. Nothing to it! For twenty-five cents, a patron was given three baseballs to knock the bottles off the barrel. They not only had to fall, but had to be completely knocked from the barrel. Doing so won the patron a stuffed animal of his or her choice. It seemed simple enough, and Tony and I took turns trying our luck before the carnival opened. Seriously? Both of us played Little League baseball. This was going to be a cakewalk! We spent the better part of an hour taking turns, and I believe Tony accomplished the feat once. His one success coupled with mine equaled one! I didn't knock all three of those bottles off the barrel one time!

The lead bottles weighed a ton, and the best one could do was cause them to fall over and come to rest on the barrel. They weren't going to roll off the barrel once they fell, because there was a one-inch lip around the edge of the barrel. One could knock the top bottle off, but getting all three to clear the barrel was next to impossible. Tony and I figured the best chance someone had was to knock each bottle off separately with each toss.

The carnival opened that evening, and our stand was one of the most popular attractions on the lot. Since there were two barrels, we had two throwers going at the same time, and we discovered that it was a tad dangerous trying to dodge the ricocheting baseballs! Because it seemed so easy to do, patrons were becoming extremely frustrated and even a bit hostile. Hey, don't kill the messenger! We only work here! We began getting some verbal abuse, and Tony and I grew a bit nervous. When the boss came by to see how things were going, some of the patrons began to take out their frustrations on him. The thing is, not all these people were strangers. Some of them were our neighbors! At the end of the night, we suggested to the boss that perhaps he might consider removing the one-inch rim from the top of the barrels. He looked at us like we were crazy!

As the week wore on, our crowds grew smaller each night. I do have to say, as a money-maker, this stand was prime! Tony and I began to feel bolder each night. No longer bothered by the slings and arrows of the crowd, we even taunted them a bit, depending, of course, on their size. We were becoming real "carnie" men, egging them on to throw another quarter on the counter and show us their stuff! I began feeling a little bit like BoBo the clown from the Allentown Fair! Then, just went we were feeling smug about our little operation, we got schooled!

The best pitcher on the Italian Club baseball team was a guy by the name of Bobby Reichel. Tony and I idolized this guy every time he took the mound for our beloved IC. Bobby showed up at the carnival one night with his wife and immediately walked over to our stand. We were in awe of this guy, and we knew we were going to feel just awful watching our hero fail with a baseball, make that three baseballs, with his wife looking on. Well, Bobby put a quarter down on the counter, picked up three baseballs and proceeded to walk back from the counter about sixty feet. My guess was that it was just about the same distance as the mound from home plate. Bang! Bobby let the first ball go and proceeded to knock all three bottles off the barrel! The guy had two more baseballs left, and for the first time all week, Tony and I had to re-set the bottles for another throw. Bang! Another ball, three bottles down! He repeated the process with the third ball and duplicated it with another quarter's worth of balls!

So much for the smug "carnies"! We were in the presence of greatness, and instead of feeling concerned about all the prizes we were turning over to Bobby, we just looked on in admiration along with the rest of the crowd that had gathered to watch this guy throw a baseball! To his credit, he gave one of the stuffed animals to his wife, another two or three to young children in the crowd, and handed the rest back to us!

Towards the end of the week, very few people stopped by our stand, and we began to grow weary of the boredom. There were only two more nights left, and we felt like we were missing all the fun. Waiting around for one or two customers all evening and having nothing to do, we began taking turns standing behind the canvas drop cloth while the other threw baseballs at the backstop trying to hit each other. When Tony became bored with that game, he picked up one of the lead bottles and let that fly. Fortunately, the bottle struck my leg instead of my skull! The boss happened to be checking on our stand at the time and decided to close the stand. It was the first time I had ever been fired, but years later Big- Hearted Benny would make it the second time!

That should have devastated us, but Tony and I were thrilled to have two nights to enjoy the carnival with our friends. We were anxious to try our luck at the ring toss, and with our newly earned money from the bottle stand, we were going to have plenty of opportunities to win the big prize. The ring toss consisted of rows of posts approximately one inch in diameter. Each post had a prize attached to it with a rubber band. One simply had to toss the ring on the post to win that prize. This game was certainly easier than the bottle game (unless you happen to be Bobby Reichel!) and most of us managed to land one of the three rings on a post. The prizes on the posts were mere trinkets, costing less than the quarter one had to shell out to play. However, the item that drew everyone to this game of chance was the magnificent hunting knife on the center post! Every kid in the neighborhood wanted that knife, including me. I'm not even sure why I wanted that knife. I didn't hunt, nor did any of my friends, but it was the prize we all knew we could win! The post on which the knife was attached was not the one-inch post that contained the plastic hand-cuffs or rubber worm. The post holding the hunting knife was approximately five inches across, and in the shape of a rectangle. My guess is that the ring was, at best, a centimeter wider than that post! The carnie operating the stand would set the ring over the post to prove to everyone that it legitimately fit, and the game was not rigged; however, throwing the ring from the angle at which we had to toss it made it virtually impossible for that ring to ever land over that post! Did that stop us from tossing all three rings at that post, thus tossing away our money?

The carnival remained open until midnight, but my parents were not about to allow me to remain there until closing. Mom and Dad had placed a table across the front of the open bakery door and were making pizzas in our hearth oven and selling them to carnival patrons. After sharing the profits with the owners of the carnival, they put the rest of the money into the coffers of the club. When they were finished for the night, it was time to head home. It was not easy for a young boy to lie in bed with his window open, looking at the lights of the Ferris wheel and hearing music and laughter a short block down the alley, but eventually I fell asleep.

The carnival provided a welcome diversion to our summer for the week, but the novelty wore off, and we were back to swimming and baseball. We were good to go until the carnies returned to the lot another year.

19.

Be Prepared

"On my honor, I will do my best to do my duty to God and my country and obey the Scout Law." That was part of the Boy Scout pledge taken by my cousin, Rod, and me when I was thirteen years old. It wasn't considered "cool" to be a Boy Scout at the time, but I really wanted to join, and Mom and Dad supported my decision. Before we could wear our scout uniforms, we had to earn our Tenderfoot badge. Once we did that, we were given our uniforms, and I still remember the first night Rod and I attended our first scout meeting in uniform. We were looking good and feeling proud!

Our house was located about six blocks from the Sacred Heart Church while Rod lived one street over. It was an easy walk to the church twice a week to attend our scout meetings. That meant passing Doc's drugstore where all our friends hung out, and they always gave us the business as we passed by in our scout uniforms. I loved my friends, and it hurt to hear their laughter as we walked by, but we felt good about ourselves every time we walked into the church to join our fellow scouts. Eventually, I was named the assistant patrol leader of our group. We were members of the Flying Eagle Patrol of Troop 50. Sounded respectable!

We went on several hikes after church on Sundays, and it was on those hikes that we were able to check off some of the requirements necessary to earn our second- class badge, but it was on our first official week of camp that really separated the men from the boys, or, at least, the Tenderfeet from the Second-Class scouts! The thought of a First-Class badge was a mere pipe dream at that stage of our scouting career!

My cousin and I arrived at Camp Trexler, the official Boy Scout camp in the Lehigh Valley and became tent-mates for the week. The tents were set up on wooden platforms and had two beds, a little table with a kerosene lamp, and two foot-lockers. In the morning, we would rise by 6:30 and hike to the mess hall where we all took turns serving breakfast. I loved being a waiter, because the waiters reported a half-hour earlier, and were served breakfast first. Camp was great, and I was ready to begin knocking down those requirements for second-class. I was going to whip right through them, and I figured my card would be checked off by the end of the week! Wrong! The second day of camp, we were told we would be earning our compass requirement that afternoon. I don't want to belabor the point, but I have been known by friends and family to have the worst sense of direction of any man alive. Using a GPS in my car as an adult does not guarantee my arriving at any destination, and I recall leaving Utah for Pennsylvania during my college days (before the invention of the GPS) stopping for dinner in Wyoming, and driving for three hours before realizing I was back in Utah!

Each scout was given a compass and a card with a list of coordinates printed on it. These coordinates, when followed correctly, would take us to various locations throughout the forest, with the final numbers leading us to one of the assigned scout masters who would then sign our card.

Taking the compass and card from one of the first-class scouts assigned to the detail, I set out into the woods, knowing I was just five co-ordinates from completing my compass-reading assignment. Lunch was to be served at the usual hour of noon, and every scout, it was assumed, would be finished with their trek and back at the mess hall ready to eat. The entire assignment was supposed to take no more than forty-five minutes to an hour; however, these foolish people had never known the likes of me during their illustrious careers in the Boy Scouts of America!

Three hours passed before the search party located me miles from the camp and nowhere near the mess hall. I wasn't scared, but I was feeling rather foolish, knowing it was only a matter of time before someone would come looking for me. Compass reading requirement, check? No! My elusive quest for that second-class badge seemed more distant than ever! At least, the humiliation was finished for the week, after all, there wasn't much more I could do wrong with only three days left before heading home. Wrong again!

Just before bedding down for the night, my cousin (who, by the way, passed his compass test with flying colors) and I were informed by our scout leader that a storm was imminent that evening, and told us to be sure to loosen the tent ropes before going to bed. He told us that rain would shrink our ropes, causing them to snap. After he left, I said to my cousin, "No way that's gonna happen!" We knew better than he, and decided to keep our ropes nice and taut, after all, we didn't want to sleep in a sagging tent!

Around two o'clock in the morning, it began to rain heavily. About an hour later, we heard a snapping sound as our tent ropes began to break. It was a windy storm, and the next thing we knew, all the lines had snapped, sending our tent flying into the woods! Left lying on our cots with the rain pouring down, we got out of the water-logged beds to search for our tent. All we needed was a flashlight; however, neither of us thought to bring one along! Two of the scout leaders took us into their tent, and in the morning, we had to walk back to our beds in soaking wet clothing while the entire camp came out of their tents to provide us with a standing ovation!

"Be Prepared" is the motto of the Boy Scouts of America! I assume that would suggest bringing a flashlight to camp. I would change the motto to "Loosen Your Tent Ropes," but it doesn't matter. My scouting career was about to take the same path as my accordion career. I wonder if Mom put my uniform in the same closet as my accordion! My departure from the scouts left me with the ignominious distinction of "Lifetime Tenderfoot"!

20.

Fight for the Purple and the Gold

I breezed into junior high school with straight A's and the delusion of intellectual superiority. The kids I was meeting for the first time were mere scholastic mortals in my eyes. My junior high career began on a rather inauspicious note. A group of ninth-grade boys, some of whom arrived at the school in their own automobiles, parking them in the faculty lot, removed my street clothes from my gym locker. After walking home at the end of the day, I gratefully entered the security of my home. Mom, seeing me walk in the house, promptly served me a baloney sandwich and asked the obligatory question, "How was your first day in junior high school?" I responded by telling her that a group of very large boys stole my clothes and sold them back to me. Using my lunch money to purchase my clothing, I hadn't had anything to eat all day, and that baloney sandwich tasted like a steak dinner!

True to the reputation of every Italian mother in our neighborhood, Mom was ready to drive to the school and deal personally with "those monsters." I couldn't imagine walking into that building the following morning knowing my mommy came there to protect me! I doubt I would have survived the second day of junior high school had she done that.

Flat tops were all the rage for boys during my junior high years. Dad cut my hair, giving me the most perfect flat top hairdo a boy could ever want. Checking out my haircut in the mirror, I left for school impressed with "the look." By the time I reached school, however, my perfect flat top had wilted considerably. I shared my dilemma with Dad, and Dad, as he usually did, solved the problem. As I was getting ready for bed, Dad came into the bathroom and handed me a jar of Crew Cut Hair Wax. He told me to rub some of the wax into my hair in the morning before brushing my hair. The stuff was amazing! My flat top stood tall and proud, and I headed to school, hatless despite the cold, winter air. Nothing was going to desecrate this masterpiece!

My desk in homeroom was located along the wall lined with radiators, and as we began opening exercises, I felt something oozing down my face and onto my shirt. My hair was melting! The wax, which had set up nicely in the cold, January air, was no match for the heat emanating from the radiators next to my desk. Returning home that day with my flat top plastered to my forehead and my shirt covered in wax stains, I immediately disposed of the infamous Crew Cut Wax!

Two life-altering events occurred that first week of junior high school. I grew up in a white Italian neighborhood containing no African Americans in my elementary school. It had been a group of black students that was responsible for my having to buy my clothing back using my lunch money on that first day, and I really wasn't certain what to make of them.

The second event was the discovery of girls! I had many female classmates in elementary school, but this was an entirely different experience. The ninth-grade girls were on the verge of womanhood. They had an air of sophistication about them and possessed street smarts unfamiliar to me. Even the seventh and eighth-grade girls were impressive. Many of these girls entered junior high school from elementary schools other than the Garfield, but even the girls with whom I attended elementary school and knew quite well seemed to have changed! Had I changed as well, or is it just the girls who become more sophisticated? At any rate, I had stepped into a new dimension in my life!

Every Wednesday during the last period of the day, students were given the option to remain in homeroom for a study hall or to purchase a dance ticket, allowing us to attend a dance in the gym. The only stipulation for those choosing the dance was that those students had to remain in the gym until 4 PM Not wanting to extend my school day an additional hour, I chose to remain in study hall. Interestingly, the only students remaining in study hall were boys! After listening to my new friends talk about how much fun they were having, I decided to plunk down my two bits for a dance ticket and find out what all the fuss was about. Like most seventh-grade boys attending the dance, I stood and watched the upperclassmen as they danced. What was the big deal?

If I were going to continue adding an hour to my school day every Wednesday, it was time for action. I decided to ask my sister to teach me how to dance, and, using her tape recorder which was filled with the popular songs of the day, thanks to her taping bandstand every afternoon, we set about launching my career as the next Fred Astaire.

Armed with this new skill, I set out on my mission. Dancing shoes at the ready, I entered the gym fully prepared to show off my moves. That's when it dawned on me. My sister, although an excellent dance instructor, never taught me how to walk up to a girl and request a dance. Just as I was settling into another Wednesday afternoon dance standing around with the rest of the guys in my class, I heard those bone-chilling words, "The next dance will be a lady's choice"! My shoes suddenly felt like bowling balls as I stared nonchalantly into space. At that moment, one of the eighth-grade girls walked over and asked me to dance. I don't really remember hearing her, due to the ringing in my ears, as she took my hand and began walking to the center of the dance floor, but I knew it was time to "man up"! I put my arm around her, and as I prepared to take her hand, she pulled me closer to her. It was at that moment that I realized how much I loved dancing!

My friend, Bobby, and I chose to walk the one mile to junior high by way of the railroad tracks. There were different routes we could have taken, but we felt this was the most direct. One morning as we were strolling alongside the tracks, the heel came off the bottom of my shoe. We were half-way to school by that time, and I really didn't want to return home to change my shoes. Examining the heel carefully, Bobby thought the nails were straight, and we could hammer it back onto my shoe.

After searching unsuccessfully for a rock large enough to serve as a hammer, Bobby suggested we set the shoe, along with the heel, on the railroad track and wait for the train. We figured that the weight of the train would press the heel back onto my shoe. Setting my shoe and heel onto the track, we waited for the train. Without fail, the train came roaring down the track, as it did every morning at 7:30 and rolled over my shoe. After it passed, we walked over to the track to pick up my shoe. We never saw that shoe again! Searching every inch of those railroad tracks and finding nothing, I resigned myself to walking the rest of the way to school wearing one shoe and one extremely dirty sock.

A few days passed before the inevitable question was asked by my parents, "Where is your other shoe?" I could not come up with any other response but the truth. After sharing my story, I waited for the explosion that never came. Mom and Dad just stood there, silently staring. Finally, they just walked away, and the incident was never mentioned again.

Gym class in junior high school was quite an adventure. Today, it is referred to as "physical education," but I cannot imagine that today's gym classes could be any more physical and certainly provide more of an "education" than ours! Our gym teacher, who doubled as our football coach, was one of the most beloved and colorful characters I've ever known.

Class consisted of three homerooms at one time, making the size of our class approximately eighty to ninety boys. There was no such thing as co-ed gym classes in those days, and it is probably just as well. A small ten foot by ten-foot mat was placed in the center of the basketball court, and the class was divided into two groups of forty-five boys on each side of the gym floor. Coach blew his whistle, and ninety boys thundered to the center of the gym and a spot on the mat. I was never a strong student of physics or geometry, but it wasn't difficult to realize that trying to fit ninety boys on a ten by ten gym mat was virtually impossible!

While we were busy clawing, pushing and punching one another, Coach was sitting in his chair reading his newspaper, his whistle clenched tightly in his teeth. After a few minutes, he blew this whistle, and anyone who did not have a portion of his body on the mat was told to line up for one whack with his paddle. He never hit us hard, and a good laugh was had by all. Surprisingly, we looked forward to that game!

In a basketball-related game, and I use that term loosely, coach (who was also the school basketball coach) set up the parallel bars on one of the foul lines and covered the bars with gym mats. Coach certainly got a lot of use out of those mats! The class was divided into two lines, and each line was given a basketball. The object of the game was to dribble the ball to the foul line, climb over the parallel bars, which were set to maximum height, dribble to the basket, shoot a lay-up and repeat the process on the way back to his team. It was a simple enough game with one extra component. Each boy could do whatever he needed to do to prevent the other team from climbing over the bars. We pushed, punched and shoved our way over the bars to return the ball to our team.

In the spring when the weather began to warm, our gym class

headed to Riverfront Park for a game of softball. Situated between the school and the park was the Wilson meat-packing plant. As we strolled through Wilson's rail yard, Coach pointed to various rocks or a stray piece of lumber and chose a few of us to pick them up to use as bases.

I remember walking through that rail yard in my football uniform on the way to the park for practice, seeing a few of the older guys climb into the open box cars. They would sit in the cars with their uniforms on and have a cigarette before practice.

During my eighth-grade year, our group of teachers approached the school district with an idea. They wanted to experiment with an "outdoor" education program. My class was one of four fortunate to take part in this experiment, approved by both the school district and the school board. It was to last for one week, and the teachers were granted the use of Camp Horseshoe, the Allentown Boys Club Camp, for the experiment. We traveled to the camp by school bus and were assigned to various bunkhouses for the week. Obviously, there were no co-ed bunkhouses! Classes were held daily just as they were during a regular school day. Science class was a no-brainer. We were given assignments to search the land for various species of insect as well as flora and fauna. In math class, we were given various problems to solve such as determining the height of a tree using certain mathematical formulas. History was a bit more difficult. Using the camp library, we were told to write a paper on the history of the camp or the surrounding county in which the camp was located. English class was my favorite. Our assignment was to write haiku poetry about the surrounding countryside and create one-act plays to be performed at the evening campfire. We enjoyed co-ed volleyball games and softball games as our gym class, and danced in the mess hall to fulfill our music education requirement. It was a great week, and the entire project was featured in the local newspaper as an "innovative approach" to education. Unfortunately, lack of funding ended the program after one year. I still think it was a great idea.

I was in a happy groove during those three years in junior high school. I made the football team as an eight-grader, enjoyed many wonderful dances, and entered ninth-grade full of confidence and enthusiasm. I enjoyed my classmates and, more importantly, my teammates, many of whom were African Americans. Life was good....and then it happened!

The years of straight A report cards, honor rolls and exemptions from final exams came to a crashing halt! I was introduced to algebra in ninth-grade and became a mere academic mortal! Frustration does not fully describe my relationship with that scholastic discipline. I hated it! My ninth-grade year continued a downward spiral culminating in a (difficult to say the words) failing grade. That F coupled with my discovery of scholastic sports and girls changed my entire outlook on the American educational system. It would take years of bad report cards and low academic self-esteem before I was able to "right the ship." More about that later.

21.

The Doctor Is In

Every kid in America has that one special gathering place he remembers from his youth. For those of us in the Italian neighborhood, that place was Doc's drugstore. I remember my Dad walking with my sister and me to Doc's on a Saturday evening. Doc had the Sunday edition of the Philadelphia Inquirer delivered to the drugstore on a Saturday and Dad like to get an early start on the news. We were always treated to an ice-cream cone or soda by Dad, and allowed to select three comic books each before heading home.

Years later, it was the gathering place for my friends and me whether we were getting ready to drive to a dance, meeting the girls with whom we hung out, or just spending a few hours socializing. We'd sidle up to the soda fountain for a lemon phosphate, a vanilla Coke, or an ice-cream cone, dispensed with the only square ice-cream dippers we had ever seen. To this day, I've never seen another.

Doc had an extraordinary display of magazines and comic books on a large rack toward the front of the store. We'd sit on the bottom rack for hours reading comics and magazines until Doc or his fountain employee walked over and told us to "Buy 'em or put 'em back!"

Two pinball machines stood in the corner and were changed every few weeks. One of our more creative friends wore his steel-toed boots he used for work when he showed up at Doc's one evening. He stood in front of one of the machines while we carefully lifted the front legs and set them on his toes. With the machine level, the pinballs never drained, which meant he could continue to play until he ran up an amazing score, putting dozens of free games on the machine. We lifted the machine off his toes and proceeded to play for free for the rest of the night. Another industrious friend from our neighborhood discovered that the backs of the machines were made of wood. Selecting a drill bit from his dad's workshop and bringing it with him to the drugstore, he began drilling a hole on the back of the machine precisely where the small wheel that registered free games was located. We took turns twisting the drill bit until we broke through the back. Using a small screwdriver, we could rotate the wheel, thus putting as many free games on the machine as we wanted. When the time came for the technician to change out the machines and empty the money boxes, he found about six nickels in the one machine. When the new machines were delivered, the wooden backs were replaced with metal!

I think the most amazing "machine" story had to come with the arrival of a shooting gallery. It replaced one of the pinball machines for a few weeks, but like all other machines, it departed rather unceremoniously never to be seen again. This "gallery" was a plastic enclosed machine with a gun mounted on the front. The back end of the gun containing the trigger extended to the outside of the machine while the barrel was inside the enclosure. The gun was on a swivel and shot wooden balls at various targets inside the machine. Different from the every-day pinball machine, it was very popular with us at first. After a week passed, we lost interest in shooting wooden balls at stationary targets, and the machine sat idle most of the evening.

It was then that one of our guys, an avid fisherman who collected grasshoppers for bait, brought a container of the hopping insects into the store. There was enough open space between the gun and the plastic casing to insert these lively critters into the shooting gallery. The grasshoppers began leaping all around inside the casing, and our interest in the machine was rejuvenated. We spent hours and plenty of our quarters attempting to hit one grasshopper, but the little guys were too fast, and to the delight of animal activists everywhere, I can honestly say that no one managed to hit a single grasshopper the entire evening. After calling it quits for the night, we headed out at closing time, and sometime during the night, every grasshopper departed the shooting gallery through the front opening. The next day there were grasshoppers jumping all over Doc's soda fountain, as well as the magazine rack and candy display. We, of course, feigned total surprise when we entered the drugstore the following evening. Eventually, every hopping bug was captured and released. No insect was harmed in the making of this story!

Most of the fountain workers at Doc's were friendly and pleasant to be around; however, Doc hired one guy who was just a bit full of himself. His self-appointed dictatorship did not fly with the guys and gals who frequented Doc's, and he continued to make enemies by exiling several of us for three days if he wasn't happy with our behavior. To say he was unpopular is an understatement. As it turned out, he was very interested in the girlfriend of a very large man who lived in an apartment above Doc's drugstore. Looking back, I'm certain that he took his infatuation with this young lady a bit too far, and one evening, while we were relaxing and reading the magazines while sipping on our Cokes, the very large fellow from upstairs walked into the drugstore. We didn't think much about it until we heard the soda jerk screaming for help. Now, let's be serious here. None of us wished bodily harm on this soda jerk, in spite of the fact that none of us liked him very much. We certainly didn't want to see him get hurt, but as I said, this was a very large man!

Chasing the soda jerk through the store, he finally caught him and picked him up. Holding our beloved jerk with one arm, the man proceeded to lift the lid to the ice-cream freezer and deposit him inside. He then sat on the lid, trapping the soda jerk! Was this man going to commit homicide by freezer? A minute later, he hopped off the lid and opened it. He actually helped our jerk out of the freezer, admonished him with a stern warning, and left the store. He never raised his voice and just smiled at us. I think I felt as cold a shiver down my spine as our soda jerk was feeling as he scraped the ice from the back of his shirt. He was a different man after that, humbler and even courteous to us. We had our beloved Doc's back!

22.

The Circuit

In 1973 Francis Ford Coppola produced the motion picture *American Graffiti*. The movie told the story of a group of friends cruising the streets of a small town in California during the final day of summer vacation in 1962. Just about every town in America has one or two streets where young adults cruised, listening to music on their car radios while socially interacting with one another. In our town, it was referred to as "doing the circuit." Our circuit began at the fairgrounds, obviously not during fair week. It continued down our downtown shopping district on Hamilton Street until we reached Eighth Street. A left turn on Eighth Street took us to Linden Street where we headed west until we arrived back at the fairgrounds. On an average night, we made this trip a few dozen times.

We made new friends, talked to old ones from one car to another, made dates and switched from one car to another as radios blared music by the Four Seasons, the Beach Boys, and the Temptations. Taking breaks from our drives, we stopped at the Ritz Barbeque located at the fairgrounds for a Coke or an ice-cream sundae.

The true "motor-heads" used that time to pop the hoods on their street rods and stare in awe and adoration at each other's engines. Most of the guys and gals in our group drove Falcons and old Chevys, and we were not interested in gazing at someone's four-cylinder engine that couldn't get out of its own way. For us, it was all about people watching, conversation, and enjoying the evening.

Bobby, one of our dear friends, who became a stand-up comedian in the local bars and clubs a few years later, found the idea of "engine worship" to be rather silly.

One night, he pulled into the fairgrounds in his beat-up Chevrolet and parked next to the muscle cars. With the motor-heads studying him intensely, he raised the hood of his car. He had the full attention of the "Heads." He casually strolled to the front of the Ritz, picked up a fully loaded trash can, walked back to his car and proceeded to dump the entire contents of the can onto his engine before dropping the hood. An extremely tense moment followed, since we were not quite certain how the motor-heads were going to respond to our friend's satirical demonstration. Silence followed, and it was deafening! Suddenly, the motor-heads burst into laughter, and we joined in, feeling a deep sense of relief. There were no arguments, no fights just laughter. It was just a normal evening in our town. People laughed, music played, and everyone enjoyed the night!

Our friend entertained us on other evenings at the fairgrounds. Reminiscent of a scene from the movie Goldfinger, in which Odd Job used his derby to chop the head off a marble statue, Bobby pulled into the fairgrounds and hopped out of his car dressed in a tuxedo and wearing a derby on his head. He proceeded to remove his derby and launch it at one of the Allentown police officers who patrolled the grounds. The hat hit the officer in the belly and fell harmlessly to the ground. The officer just looked at him, shook his head and said, "Bobby."

We lived in an innocent time then, and I honestly believe that no longer exists in this country!

23.

Pigs and Salami

Very little time seemed to pass between adventures where our group of guys was concerned. From the moment the Brahma bull that had escaped from the Allentown Fair was captured on Tony's street, we had already moved on to the next escapade.

Rumors of an albino lady ghost spread through the town like wildfire. Stories of her sightings had even made the local newspaper, and had been reported on Philadelphia TV news stations. Witnesses told stories of seeing her "floating" above the street, and several people were certain they had seen her heading to Allentown's reservoir at an amazing rate of speed. It was all the information we needed, and we were off to the reservoir armed with ropes and flashlights on our mission to capture the "ghost lady"!

I remember asking myself at the time, "Do I really believe this lady exists?" Did anyone in our group believe in this ghost? Were we really that naive? Could there really be an albino lady ghost who, apparently, traveled at the speed of light? I was pretty sure no one in our group expected to find her, let alone capture her, but it was an "adventure" we couldn't pass up. Ironically, we were not the only group of guys in the reservoir's woods that evening. Dozens of kids, both guys and gals, armed with everything from large sacks, baseball bats (were they planning to club this woman?) and ropes, trudged through the darkened forest in search of the ghost lady.

Shouts of "I see her!" and "She's over there!" pierced the evening air, but many hours later, we walked wearily to our cars. To no one's surprise, our "floating ghost" was never found, and the local paper moved onto other stories. We also moved on to our next adventure, and it was a beauty!

Movies were an integral part of our lives back then. Our group not only watched a movie, we experienced it. In the early sixties, we went to see the film *Ocean's Eleven*. Sitting in the balcony of the Colonial Theater, we were transfixed as Frank Sinatra and the rest of the Rat Pack pulled off the greatest heist of the century, robbing all the major casinos in Las Vegas at one time while Dean Martin and Sammy Davis Jr. sang "Ain't Love a Kick in the Head" and "Ee-o Eleven"!

It was summertime, and we planned one of our many picnics at the bungalow owned by Rollie's dad and uncle. The bungalow was located outside the city and contained everything we needed, including a pool, for the girls in our gang and us to enjoy a fun, summer afternoon. We got together with the girls to make plans for the picnic, and, as it always does, the subject of food was raised. The typical menu of hot dogs and hamburgers was brought up, but deciding to go a different route, Rollie had an idea. It was at that moment that the wheels of our next adventure were set in motion as Rollie announced to the gang that we would be having a pig roast!

Allow me to say at this point of the story, that not one of us had ever roasted a pig, nor did we possess the equipment to roast a pig. The most important point to be made, however, was that we didn't have a pig, nor did we have an inkling as to how to set about procuring a pig! Details!

It just so happened that a few miles beyond the city limits of Allentown, a farm existed that raised perfect porkers for market. What did a pig cost? Did it come ready for roasting? Was the proper roasting equipment included with the purchase of the pig? None of these questions required an answer because the boys who watched Danny Ocean and his gang rob seven casinos knew what we had to do. If Frank Sinatra could rob seven casinos, surely our group of guys could heist one pig from Chun's Pig Farm! And so, the adventure began.

Waiting until sunset, we gathered in the parking lot of the Italian Club where my father's bakery trucks were parked. My cousin secured the keys to one of the trucks from the bakery and slid behind the wheel. I always wondered how he managed to get inside the bakery, but I figured it was best to let that go. The rest of us climbed into the bed of the panel truck, and we set off on our mission.

While Ron drove, the rest of us passed around a tin of black Kiwi shoe polish and proceeded to smear the paste on our faces. Armed with ropes, baseball bats, and a large empty flour sack from the bakery, we journeyed to Chun's farm while Tony led us all in a rousing rendition of "Ee-O Eleven"! The Rat Pack was primed to strike again!

Parking the truck about a mile from the farm, we continued on foot with Rollie, our fearless leader out in front. As we approached the farm, Rollie ordered his troops to "hit the ground"! It had rained the day before, leaving us to lie in a bed of mud. Gripping a hunting knife in his teeth, Rollie began crawling toward the farm, his troops following closely behind. We slithered through the mud for several hundred yards before reaching the out-lying fence of the farm. As we approached the fence, a low, groaning sound pierced the night air. We froze - a team of muddied statues holding our breaths while waiting orders from our commanding officer. Was it a pig? A frog? We never did find out.

While we waited, a discussion ensued. Tony asked, "How are we going to kill the pig?" That question led to a more important one. WHO was going to kill the pig? At that moment, it became clear to me and everyone else in our group. Not even Frank Sinatra himself was going to kill a pig that night!

Needing to save face, we convinced ourselves that the farm was much too fortified for us to get close to a pig, and it was best to call a halt to our mission. We trudged back to the truck in silence like the Rat Pack did after learning their loot had been cremated along with Richard Conte's body! Our picnic, as always, was a huge success. The next day was filled with sunshine, music, and laughter pierced the air as we swam in the spring-fed pool of the bungalow, and dined on fabulous sandwiches made with salami from Rollie's Italian market. "Eee-O Eleven"!

24.

Dreaming of Donna Reed

As the August weather heated up, driving kids to their favorite swimming hole, it was also time for football practice to begin. I loved and respected all my high school football coaches, but they were old school. Drinking water was a no-no. It made us soft, and the only way to toughen us was to drive us to dehydration! We never questioned our coaches about that or assigned blame in any way. Every school in the Lehigh Valley practiced using that same policy. It was especially difficult for us because our practice field sat next to one of Allentown's public pools, and we had to watch kids splashing in the cool water of the pool and eating snow cones the entire time we were running drills and swallowing dust created by the lack of lawn after two or three days of practice.

One morning, we were told to report to the gym before heading outside to the practice field. It had been decided by some "higher up" that it was best to have every player's ankles wrapped before each practice. This was not a bad idea; however, unlike today's high school programs with a staff of trainers and a training room outfitted with all the modern equipment, most schools, including ours, had a small training room complete with bandages, a few rolls of tape and tubs of something known as Atomic Balm, a red paste with a core temperature of molten lava! One of our coaches would stand outside the door of the training room each morning and glare at anyone who might have considered entering the room to see Doc, our trainer. That intimidating stare turned most of us around, figuring it was not a good idea to seek treatment.

OK, so there we were in the gym, awaiting instructions from a trainer who must have been circulating through all the school districts to show us how we were going to wrap our ankles by ourselves! Issued two ankle wraps apiece, we paid close attention to his instructions. Using one of our players, the instructor demonstrated the proper way to wrap one's ankle to provide strength and stability to said ankle, thus eliminating sprains from occurring. We spent the next half hour practicing this technique before we were instructed to wrap our ankles and hustle out to the practice field. The result, if not disastrous, was hilarious! Guys walked across the street from the school on their way to the practice field with two feet of wrap dragging behind them. We began stepping on each other's wraps as they trailed along behind us. It was decided the next day that there would be fewer injuries without these wraps than with them, and they vanished from our lockers never to be seen or heard from again.

August practices were grueling, and at the end of one morning session, as we were heading back inside to shower, one of the guys was on all fours returning his breakfast to the grass. One of our coaches walking by, noticed this, and replied, "It's the only way to die, son, for your school." We all survived August, and it was time to begin the school year.

I was one of a few guys fortunate to have my own car. It belonged to my sister and me, but she was away at college, so I got to use it most of the time. Living on the north side of Allentown while our high school was located on the east side of the city, I picked up many guys on my way to school. It got to a point that, before we even arrived, there were so many guys in my car that we could not close the doors. Forget seat belts! I had to go around street corners carefully to prevent anyone from falling out of the back seat. The end guys had to hold the doors closed and hang on for dear life!

Occasionally, we decided to pass the school and head to the diner for some breakfast before heading to class. The fact that we had already eaten breakfast did not enter our thinking. One morning, as we dined on pancakes and eggs, Shorty, our milkman, walked into the diner and spotted us sitting at the back table. He apparently wasted no time before driving to Dad's bakery to let him know where his son was. Ten minutes later, Dad came thundering into the diner, took one look at the back table, and shouted loudly enough for every patron to hear, "Get your rear-end outta that seat and over to school!" I swear there were other patrons that got up to leave before realizing they weren't even in school anymore.

There were two public high schools in Allentown. Ours was located on the east side of town while the original high school was located on the west end of town. Sandwiched between the two public buildings was Allentown Central Catholic High School. Rivalry between the two public schools was intense with not much love lost between the two. The biggest football game of the season for both schools was the Allen-Dieruff game. Today, if one attends a high school football game, he or she may see a few thousand fans in the stands, but during the sixties, an Allen-Dieruff game played in the shared school district stadium had crowds of over sixteen thousand people!

During fair week that year, one of the local radio stations was doing a live broadcast from the midway to promote the fair. The disc jockey interviewed people as they strolled through the midway and happened to stop one of our players for a chat. Eventually, the conversation worked its way to the Dieruff football team. When asked what kind of season he expected us to have, he replied, "I don't know, but we are gonna kick Allen's butt!" With that, the gauntlet had been thrown down. Emotions and excitement always picked up during game week, and the morning of game day, a bunch of us drove over to the west side of town, skipping first period. Upon arrival, some of the football players entered the school, something that wouldn't even be allowed to happen in today's world, and we distributed newspapers headlining Dieruff's victory over Allen to the students in study hall. The proctors of the study hall immediately chased us from the building and out into the street. Several of the guys jumped in my car to make our escape only to find my car would not start. With both proctors and angry students gaining on my car, one of the other guys pulled his car up to the back of mine and began pushing me down the street. We had escaped! Unfortunately, the tail light on my car was demolished! Another confrontation with my dad loomed on the horizon! I drove that poor man crazy!

As we arrived at the parking lot of Dieruff, the first thing we saw were the tombstones with our names on them stretching across our practice field. While we were spending time at Allen, the west side guys were visiting our side of town! In addition to the head stones, the Allen guys had turned two dozen canaries loose in our building. Perhaps I failed to mention that Allen's mascot was a canary. That, unto itself, was fodder for harassment!

Entering the building, we were told to report to Mr. Bear's office immediately! Mr. Bear was our assistant principal and a pretty tough dude. His first words to us before sending us to class were, "Catch 'em." We spent the next hour chasing down the canaries and took them to Mr. Bear's office. While everyone was sitting in their classes, an announcement came over the PA system. It was Mr. Bear, who told everyone to listen as he held the microphone up to the cage, and everyone was treated to chirping over the PA. A huge cheer went up throughout the school. Game on.

In addition to the tombstones and canaries, the Allen guys committed one grievous offense. They had kidnapped Kiska, our beloved Husky who was the mascot of our school. A notification went out to Allen that, unless the dog was returned, there would be no game that night. Kiska was returned unharmed, and it was time for the pep rally to close the school day.

At the end of the pep rally, students departed the gym to find several cars in the middle of the street. Allen students drove to the east side to harass the student body. Big mistake! Dieruff students immediately blocked both sides of the street and began dancing on the roofs and hoods of the cars, denting them significantly. The football players were in seclusion by this time, safely away from any trouble. While we lay on the wrestling room mats listening to music and relaxing before heading to the stadium, several Allentown police officers entered the room stating that we were going to be arrested for the destruction of property. Game on? Perhaps not. Once it was made clear that we had not been involved in the damage to the automobiles, everyone calmed down, and it was time to head to the stadium.

One of our coaches called us aside before boarding the bus to the stadium. He let us know how unhappy he was with those of us who made the trip to Allen that morning. I should point out that only a small number of players made that trip. Those were the guys he was addressing. He told us he didn't condone that type of behavior, but if we were going to do something as immature as that, putting the entire team in jeopardy, we better win the game! A great ending to this story would be that we throttled Allen, and all was forgiven. We lost! Not only did we lose, but we were a four and two team, and Allen was winless. The player who predicted our victory to the local radio station didn't win very many points with the coach either.

Monday's practice was always an easy one. We looked at game film, and the coaches went over the scouting report of our next opponent, after which we headed home. Our routine didn't waiver. Those players who were not part of the "visitation" to Allen followed the usual protocol. Those of us who made the trip to Allen, not so much. We were told to suit up and meet Coach on the practice field in fifteen minutes. It was a cold, rainy, miserable afternoon when we stepped onto the field, and our coach was smiling. None of us took that as a good sign. We began with one hundred push-ups. When we got to ninety-nine, he told us we were not doing them correctly and we needed to start over. It was the same for our sit-ups, and then we lined up at the goal line for crab drill. Crab drill meant crawling on our hands and feet for whatever distance the coach deemed necessary. If our knees touched the field, we were told to begin again. The distance Coach deemed necessary didn't surprise us. It was one hundred yards, at which time, we turned around and repeated the journey back to the other goal line. The rain continued to fall, and we continued to drill until, mercifully, our coach sent us inside. Everyone had gone home, and the locker room was empty. We began to remove our rain-soaked uniforms which were muddied beyond recognition when Coach came in and told us to sit on the floor. He reminded us that part of Monday's practice included watching the game film. As the film, painful to watch, by the way, wound down to its conclusion, we began to rise and head to the showers. No! We sat through the entire game film two more times before unloading our gear and heading to the showers.

I arrived home around eight-thirty, and my dinner was on the table wrapped in plastic as it always was during the season. Dad was downstairs watching TV, and Mom was still at work. Removing the wrap from my plate, I dug into the very cold, very hard plate of meatloaf. I hit the sack right afterwards and slept the sleep of the dead. For one moment in the morning, I considered staying home from school, but I didn't dare! After school, it was practice as usual, and we were expected to hustle like every other player on that field. We did, without complaint. No one said a word about yesterday's "practice," and as far as we were concerned, it was over. To no one's surprise, we throttled our next opponent. Somebody had to pay!

A few weeks later, we were playing Easton on another cold, rainy, Friday night. Easton was a powerhouse that season, and they were beating us up badly. We went into the locker room down 30 to 0, and waited for our coaches. They never came in. We sat there, staring at one another for the entire half-time. Finally, the door opened, and one of the coaches stuck his head inside and said, "Let's go, ladies." Fired up from that embarrassing slight to our manhood, we went out and proceeded to lose the game 47 to 6!

The scene takes place in the Stone family living room. Jeff Stone is sitting with his mom and dad holding a cat that has followed him home. He wants to keep the cat, but his dad, Doctor Alex Stone decides to hold a family meeting before a decision is reached. Jeff's mom, played by Donna Reed and his sister, played by Shelley Fabares, are also involved in the decision-making process.

I wake up! Where am I, and why am I dreaming of Donna Reed? Gazing around the unfamiliar room, I begin to panic. I begin to shout, and a nurse enters the room. "It's OK," she tells me. "You are in the hospital." The rest of the story does not come from my memory, but rather from the accounts of my teammates and family members.

After catching a pass in a high school football game, and taking a clean, but violent hit, I returned to the huddle. Turning to one of my teammates, I asked him who we were playing, and he looked at me rather strangely. When we broke the huddle, rather than walking towards the line of scrimmage, I walked in the opposite direction. Quickly calling a time out, one of my coaches came onto the field, took me by the hand, and walked me to the sideline. After returning to the school, one of the coaches gave me a note to give to my parents. I, somehow, left the locker room and was found wandering the halls of the school in my underwear. Fortunately, it was a Friday night, and the halls were empty. One of the coaches drove me home, and when he walked me into the house, my family was gathered around the television set watching (you guessed it) the Donna Reed Show! After returning home, I was unable to recollect anything about the events of that evening. The last thing I remembered was tying the laces on my football shoes. The doctor told my parents that I needed to skip the final two games of the season to heal properly. He wanted me to rest and not take any chances of getting another blow to the head. Three days later, while jumping over an electric cord in our kitchen, I hit my head on a wooden archway, went down for the count, and was rushed to the emergency room. After having the top of my head shaved, I received fifteen stitches in my scalp. Apparently, I would have been better off finishing the season. At least I would have been wearing a helmet! I'm not sure if Jeff Stone was ever allowed to keep the cat!

25.

Hoss and the Strawberry Pie

The crown jewel of downtown Allentown's shopping district during the late 1950s and 1960s was Hess's department store. The first thing to catch a person's eye, especially at night, was the elaborate forty-five-foot sign over the front entrance. Each letter in the word "Hess" was seven feet high, and the entire sign was illuminated with 2,250 light bulbs and neon lighting. The three-sided sign was visible to not only those entering the store, but to east-bound and west- bound traffic as well. The sign was turned on for the first time on December 23, 1947 in time for the Christmas holiday. It rivalled anything Times Square had to offer and dazzled everyone who passed by.

Hess's was five floors of wonder and awe for the people who shopped there. From its exquisite chandeliers, suspended from the ceiling of each level, to the stunning Hess's models who strutted so elegantly throughout the store, Hess's was truly a remarkable work of man.

Statues of the presidents stood against the columns of each floor as projectors, mounted on the ceilings, showed images of each presidential face. As the film rolled, each president spoke to the shoppers about his exploits as Commander-in- Chief of our great nation.

A major attraction to the store was The Patio. Hess's Patio was world-renowned for its cuisine, and no one who spent time in the store ever passed up the opportunity to enjoy a piece of Hess's strawberry pie! A favorite of so many of the stars of motion pictures and TV that visited the store, the pie stood over six inches high and contained four pounds of berries. Celebrities of all walks of life came to see Hess's department store and enjoy a piece of that pie. The Patio lost twenty-thousand dollars a year, but owner, Max Hess, believed that it was a major draw to shoppers and worth the loss.

Stars like Johnny Carson, Zsa Zsa Gabor, Rock Hudson, Sophia Loren and countless others could be seen walking the floors of Hess's. Even George Reeves, star of the television series, "Superman" made an appearance, and the entire cast of "Bonanza" could be seen dining on a slice of strawberry pie at the Patio. The great Phillip Petit, France's popular daredevil walked a tightrope stretched from Hess's fifth floor across the street to a neighboring department store. My friends and I spent countless hours walking through the five levels of Hess's, gazing at the gorgeous models and spending our parents' hard-earned cash!

Our friend, Bobby, he of the infamous "Odd Job" stunt at the fairgrounds, continued his comedic ways in Hess's. The Patio was very popular with all the shoppers, but especially attractive to the higher end of society. Politicians and sports figures joined celebrities at the Patio. It was a place "to be seen." Bobby, who worked at one of the retail men's stores in town, walked into The Patio, dressed to the nines in a three-piece suit, carrying a very expensive-looking briefcase. Sitting alone at one of the tables, his gold cufflinks sparkling in the light, he ordered a beverage and took out a small key from his vest pocket. At this point, he had the attention of every VIP in the restaurant. Setting his briefcase on the table, he proceeded to unlock it and lift the lid, taking a pile of comic books out and setting them on the table! As he began reading his comic books, the patrons turned back to their lunch. Obviously, this man was no one of importance. It was just one more satirical statement being made by our dear friend.

As sophisticated as the store was with its never-ending stream of celebrities and its famous pie, Hess's was a department store that catered to the average working man and woman of our fair city. Like most stores, Hess's held an annual clearance sale. The thing that made Hess's sale uniquely different from other stores was its presentation. Hess's published two full-page advertisements in the local newspaper not only announcing the date of the clearance sale but also listing every single item for sale by price as well as quantity. In some cases, the item's quantity was listed as "one."

I was sixteen when I drove to downtown Allentown and found a parking space on the street, several blocks from the store. Hess's later constructed an enormous parking deck; however, at that time, parking was available where one could find a space. I walked to the store and joined the massive crowd waiting for the doors to open at nine a.m. I was on a mission. I knew the stereo system was located on the fourth floor, and I also knew that only one was available. Skipping the elevators and escalators, already crowded with shoppers, I chose instead to sprint up the stairs to the fourth floor. Having done a reconnaissance mission a few days earlier, I knew exactly where the stereo was located. As I reached out and wrapped my arms around the turntable, I saw another set of arms approaching from the side. Before I knew what was happening, someone lifted the two speakers from the table. I had been ambushed! Holding the turntable tightly to my chest, I turned to see a man in his early twenties clutching the precious speakers. We stared each other down like two gunfighters in a scene from Gunsmoke. I took pride in being a seasoned veteran of the Hess's clearance sales, but I had let my guard down. It was at that moment when the man tried to pull the turntable from my arms! I was about to lose this stereo system to a total stranger, someone who probably didn't even appreciate music as much as I did. We struggled for what seemed an eternity. It became a battle of wills, neither one of us conceding defeat!

Suddenly, the guy just stopped wrestling, handed me the two speakers, and said, "You want this more than I do." I piled the two speakers on top of the turntable, and not taking any chances, paid and quickly took the stairway four floors to the main entrance. I hurried down the two blocks to my car, hoping I wouldn't get mugged for my stereo on the way by some music-loving street person! I drove away in the immortal words of Jack London's book, Call Of The Wild, as the "dominant, primordial beast who had made his kill and found it good."

26.

Tony and the Rock

Saturday night meant Castle Rock! Most of the time, we all met at Doc's and headed to Dorney Park from there, but many Saturday evenings I walked to Tony's house and we rode to Castle together. Before talking about Castle Rock, I think it's time to talk a little bit about Tony. I've mentioned him often in this book, and for good reason. The term BFF didn't exist when we were growing up, but if ever it applied to anyone in my life, it had to be Tony. I loved every one of the guys and gals in our gang, but Tony was special. He was my best friend.

Our parents were very close friends, and often got together on Saturday nights for a game of canasta. Whether they played at our house or Tony's house, the kids were always part of the evening. My sister Anita and Tony's sister Rosie listened to their music and talked about boys, while Tony and I played together. The night usually began with dinner, and with both our moms being excellent cooks, the meal was always fantastic. As the evening ended, and the canasta game ended, it was time for Tony and me to make our pitch. Either we appealed to my parents to let Tony sleep over or, if we were at Tony's house, we petitioned his mom and dad to allow me to spend the night. Either way, we were usually successful, and I believe our parents knew what was coming before we approached them, and they gave us a tough time, knowing they were going to say "yes" anyway!

In those days, we were inseparable. We fished together, rode our identical Invicta English bikes to the park either to swim at the Jordan pool or to find a baseball game. As we grew older, nothing changed. Best friends forever, as the saying goes! Tony is two years older than I, and I idolized the guy. He was my protector. One evening while ice-skating on a public arena in Bethlehem, I was stopped by two thugs as I was skating around the rink. They decided for some reason to give me a difficult time and wouldn't allow me to continue skating. At that moment, Tony skated up to the three of us, got in their faces and said something to them. I don't know what he said, but their faces grew ashen, and they skated away. During the Castle Rock years of our lives, I can only say that the man was my idol! He was the trend-setter in our group, and everyone tried to emulate him. He was first to show up with a campus haircut, and we were quick to follow his lead. The guy was all about style, and he always looked fantastic as we readied ourselves for a night at the "Rock." He wore the right shoes, dressed the right way, and always walked with an air of confidence. Tony tells everyone he meets, even today, that I was his "bait" to get girls because I was so good looking... his words, not mine. The truth is, that guy needed no help in that department. The girls were crazy about him, and I believe that the opposite is true. I figured hanging around Tony was the best thing I could do to meet girls.

Tony - he was the "man"!

If all of this were not enough, the man could flat out dance!

Nobody at Castle Rock could out dance this guy! He and one of the gals in our gang by the name of Pat Yurkovitz entered a twist contest, and to no one's surprise, won first place. That contest won them a trip to the famous Peppermint Lounge in New York!

My dad loved Tony, and Tony had tremendous respect for Dad as well. If Tony and I were going to a movie, he would suggest taking my dad along. We took him with us to see the movie Irma la Douce and he enjoyed it completely. Every so often, Tony and I would drive out to the west end of town and rent Honda 50's from Kitto's Honda rentals. We rode them through the streets and headed to our local parks, where we motored through the park trails and paths. Once again, Tony said, "Why don't we take your dad along?" It happened to be my dad's 50th birthday, and we told him we had a birthday treat for him. Wearing his mirrored sunglasses, which made him look like the armed guard from *Cool Hand Luke*, Dad mounted his Honda and off he went like Peter Fonda in *Easy Rider*! We headed to the south side of Allentown and into Cedar Crest College, an all-women's college in south Allentown near the Rose Garden. Charging full speed ahead, we raced into the middle of a women's gym class and were immediately pursued by the campus police! Dad had many great birthdays in his life, but I know that birthday was one of his most memorable!

As years passed, Tony and I saw less of each other due to two totally different career paths, but one evening, I had stopped over to my parents' house, and there were Tony's parents and my mom and dad playing canasta. I almost began to cry because they, too, had lost touch over the years. Seeing them sitting there, laughing, as though a day had never passed between them, I was inspired. I wrote Tony a letter (there were no computers or smart phones in those days). I told him about our parents, and I stressed the importance of not letting anymore time lapse between us. Tony was a police detective living near Philadelphia at the time, and I drove to his house where we ended up having dinner and re-uniting our past. Unfortunately, we lost touch a second time, but a few years later, met for dinner with his brother and sister and their significant others at Louie's Italian Restaurant in Allentown. From that moment on, we have remained close. Tony had a terrible illness a few years ago, but no surprise to me, he beat the illness with the same cool he exhibited on the dance floor. We continue to keep in touch, and still enjoy visits today. As with our parents, it's as though a day has never passed between us.

As I said before I reminisced about my friendship with Tony, Saturday night meant Castle Rock! We spent many nights going to dances all over the Lehigh Valley, but nothing compared to our Saturday nights at Castle Rock! Unless someone was suffering from a terrible illness or a psycho attack in the shower (I'll explain later) he or she was at the "Rock." Castle Rock was formerly a ballroom named Castle Gardens and located in Dorney Park, Allentown's very popular amusement park. It opened in 1923, and our parents danced there to the sound of the big bands during the thirties and forties. It was a huge dance hall with eight thousand square feet of maple hardwood on which to dance. After the demise of the big bands, Castle became a roller rink for several years before returning to its original venue as a dance hall, our dance hall!

To appeal to a younger crowd during the sixties, the name changed from Castle Gardens to Castle Rock, and rock we did! For four hours every Saturday night, we danced to records spun by local DJs like Kerm Gregory and Jay Sands. Performers like Frankie Avalon, Fabian, Sam Cooke, The Fleetwoods, Paul Anka, and Annette Funicello were just a few of the stars who performed at the "Rock." We danced from eight o'clock until ten and had a twenty-minute intermission before returning for more music and dancing until midnight!

One of the things that stood out to me then, which I am still reminded of today, was the dress! Nobody was there in jeans or cut-offs, no T-shirts or sweatshirts. They weren't permitted. The amazing thing is, we loved to dress up! Every girl wore a dress, and the guys were decked out in either a suit or sport coat. Ties were mandatory. Everyone looked sharp! It was our one night during the week to shine, and as I said earlier in this chapter, nobody did it better than Tony!

Entering Castle, the first thing the guys did was hit the men's room. Every guy was combing his hair and splashing his face with the complimentary bottles of Old Spice available by the sinks. It wasn't easy to impress a girl with one's after shave because we all smelled the same!

When it was time for intermission, everyone headed outside, weather permitting. During the summer, we would head over to the roller coaster dressed in our suits and ride two or three times. In those days, we were allowed to remain on the coaster at the end of the ride and do it again. The girls, dresses and all, rode the coaster with us. We played Skee- Ball, ate French fries and rode on the merry-go-round before heading back to Castle.

I began going to Castle when I was in eighth-grade, and unlike Tony, was still a little shy around girls. One evening, during a lady's choice, I was asked to dance by a lovely, young lady. After dancing with her several times that evening, I found out later that she was a senior at Liberty High School in Bethlehem. When I returned home that night and took off my sport coat, I found a slip of paper in the pocket with her name and phone number on it and quickly flushed it down the toilet! I was in over my head! The next Saturday night, Tony called to tell me to meet him at his house around seven-thirty, and I told him I might not go to Castle that night. After the shock wore off, Tony asked me why I would ever miss a night at the "Rock." I told him about the note in my pocket and he just laughed and told me not to be late. I saw her again that night, and even danced with her a few times before telling her I was in eighth-grade. She moved on to someone else, and I felt relieved, although, I must say, my ego took a little hit that night!

One summer evening as Tony and I crossed the bridge on our way to Castle, we heard loud voices coming from one of the showboats just about to pass Castle. A second glance told us something was not quite right. The boat, filled with patrons of Dorney Park, was sinking! By the time we walked over to the bank, the boat had sunk to the bottom. That might sound disastrous, but the pond was only about two feet deep and came to rest on the bottom without any of the water spilling onto the deck. The problem is that the people on the boat were not dressed for a swim, and there really was no way to reach the shore without stepping into the pond. Many of the guys on the boat had already done so, but the ladies were a bit more hesitant. It was then that Tony sprang into action. Taking off his expensive, Italian shoes and rolling the legs of his suit pants as high as he could, he stepped into the water. Not knowing any better, I followed him into the pond after removing my shoes and socks and rolling up my pant legs as well. We proceeded to carry a few of the girls to shore, making certain we found the prettiest ones to rescue first! While this was going on, their boyfriends and husbands looked on sheepishly. Many years later, while visiting my mom in her assisted living home, there was an announcement that a lecture on the history of Dorney Park, complete with slides, was to take place in their living center. Mom and I went down to hear the lecture and watch the slides. The gentleman giving the lecture got to the part when the showboat sank and told the residents that "two young men waded into the water and carried several of the ladies to shore." He added that the two men made sure to carry the pretty ones out first! I stopped his lecture long enough to let him know that I was one of those two guys. Everyone in the room had a good laugh!

During the winter months, there was still an intermission at the dance, but obviously, no one could go outside. One Saturday evening, the snow was falling heavily. Because three sides of the building were all windows, we were able to see how much snow had fallen and even considered leaving the dance early. That thought lasted two minutes. None of us were going to miss a minute of the "Rock." Everyone stood on the side of the dance floor, hanging out with his or her respective gangs as police officers walked around the floor, making sure everyone who was not dancing kept to the sides of the dance floor. I was standing with our friends, talking to one of the girls in our gang when the officer walked by and gave me a little shoulder bump to move me to the side of the floor. After he passed, my cousin Ron said to me, "You don't have to put up with that. The next time he walks by and bumps you, bump him right back!" I had no intention of provoking this man, who was about six-feet-four and two hundred and twenty pounds! I wouldn't have bothered to do anything because it was no big deal, and I just moved back a foot or two. When he came around again, my cousin, yes, the same cousin who put the bakery truck in neutral, purposely stepped out onto the dance floor a bit. When the police officer walked past, he gave Ron a little push to move him back. He, in turn, pushed the officer, and the next thing we knew, the cop had him by the collar and was dragging him outside. He had arrived at the dance with a date, and he called to her, "We gotta go!" She looked at him and told him she wasn't going anywhere until the dance was over. There were still almost two hours remaining in the dance, and my cousin spent them stewing in his Packard waiting for his date!

Before my sister's gang had moved on to college and was still going to Castle, a friend of hers and I were talking about someone we both knew. He couldn't picture him, and I told him that my sister had a picture of the guy in her wallet. We walked over to the bleachers where people sat when they were tired of standing or dancing, and I found my sister's purse, took out her wallet and showed him the picture. Before we knew what was happening, two police officers escorted us to the park office where we were held for taking a wallet out of someone's purse. There were no cell phones and no way to reach my sister, but fortunately for us, one of her friends saw what happened and told my sister. She and my sister left the dance and walked to the park office to help. I might point out that they didn't leave immediately. They had to dance The Stroll before they could come to the rescue! We were cleared and allowed back into the dance with the stern warning to "stay out of other people's purses!"

My sister's gang always ended an evening at Castle Rock with a trip to Marco's, which was a small hot dog shop on Gordon Street in Allentown. Taking our lead from them, we went to Marco's and dined on hot dogs, French fries and chocolate milk before heading home. After Sis's gang moved on, we decided it was time for us to establish our own tradition. We began heading to Haney's Pig Stand on Union Boulevard, a much more sophisticated establishment, where we dined on hot dogs and French fries, but we varied our menu by ordering Cokes instead, and rebels that we were, added pizza to our dining table. Some of the guys arrived earlier because others had to drop their dates off before heading for a bite to eat. No, they weren't cheapskates! The girls had to be home right after the dance. Dates were a whole lot cheaper then!

The Christmas holiday had just come to an end, and we were gathered at Haney's for a bite to eat after the dance. Afterwards, we headed to the parking lot and a drive home. The lot next to Haney's had been used to sell Christmas trees and was now empty. Three pipes, presumably used to support Christmas trees a few weeks earlier, protruded from the ground. I assume the lot had been filled with these pipes and for some reason, these three remained behind. As Tony and I were getting into his car, my cousin began backing up his Packard to turn around. In his defense, it was a dark evening, and there were no lights in either lot. Traveling a little too far and perhaps a bit too fast, he backed over the first pipe. As he did, the pipe, rather than remaining flat on the ground, sprung partially back up and impaled the Packard. Ron was unable to drive forward and the pipe dug into the undercarriage of his car. He was in a bind, and we could not leave without assisting him, or at the very least, offering him some advice. Tony, just as he had suggested to the man in front of our church on Christmas Eve to drive his car down the sidewalk, told my cousin to "go backwards." I guess it made sense; after all, he certainly wasn't going forward! Backing up the Packard, he went over another pipe. Now, there were two pipes under his car basically holding it off the ground! There was one pipe left. After trying one more time unsuccessfully to pull forward, Ron backed up again. To no one's surprise, there were now three pipes under his car, and he wasn't going anywhere! It was then that Tony told him to do the only thing he could do, and that was to continue to drive in reverse until he was clear of all the pipes. The racket that ensued brought Marvin and Betty, the proprietors of Haney's, out of the diner and into the rear lot. We assured them that everything was fine, and we were heading home. The Packard was free! However, we found my cousin's oil pan lying on the ground. Locking his car, Ron hopped in Tony's Buick, and we drove home.

I mentioned earlier in this chapter on the "Rock" that no one missed Castle unless he or she was suffering a terrible illness or experienced a psycho moment in the shower. I missed two consecutive Saturdays at Castle, and it wasn't due to a terrible illness! I was getting ready for the dance and had my best-looking suit on for the evening. As I looked down at my shoes, there was a problem. These babies needed a shine! Digging out the shoeshine kit from my dad's workshop, I set about polishing my shoes. When I finished, I just didn't feel like they were "popping" the way they should. They needed a good buffing, but that would take a fine piece of clean cloth, and the rags in that shine box were just not going to do the job. I went upstairs to my dad's underwear drawer and found the perfect undershirt to use. It was clean, soft, and pristine! It should have been; it was brand-new. I needed to be able to grip it properly, and there was just too much material in the way. Not a problem. Using my mom's sewing scissors, I cut off the perfect buffing cloth and used it put a shine on those shoes one could shave by.

As I was busily showering and humming some of the songs I knew would be playing at the "Rock" that night, I looked up just in time to see a shadow looming on the other side of the shower curtain. Suddenly, an arm was raised holding something that looked like Norman Bates' knife in the famous shower scene from Psycho. With that, the curtain was pulled back, and Dad stood there holding a piece of my mom's vacuum cleaner pipe in his hands and a very dangerous look in his eyes! He began to pummel me with the pipe. In his defense, my dad never struck me hard, and I adored the man, but he was furious! My injuries weren't sustained by the vacuum cleaner pipe, but rather from the fact that, as I tried to run from the blows, I kept running into the shower walls! It was a very small shower. OK, I deserved Dad's wrath. The shirt was brand-new and still had the tags on it, but the punishment was severe! Not the beating, but rather the knowledge that I would not be allowed to attend a dance at Castle Rock for one month! Dad might as well have burned my dancing shoes! That would have been devastating, since they had the best shine I had ever seen on a pair of shoes!

The following Saturday night, Mom was working, and Dad and I sat in the basement watching Gunsmoke. I died a slow death that night, but Dad was not about to give in. Tony, in his ultimate wisdom, didn't even try to call. He knew better. The following week was pretty much status-quo, Gunsmoke and whatever followed. My mind was elsewhere. I was sitting on the sofa during the third Saturday of my banishment from Castle when Dad came down and said, "You'd better hurry if you're going to the dance." I have no idea what divine intervention had taken place, but I wasn't taking any chances. I bolted from the sofa, took a shower, called Tony and put on my best suit. The shoes still looked better than any shoes I had ever seen!

27.

Green Street

Three blocks south of our neighborhood, Green Street intersected with Jordan Street, still a very important part of the Italian section of Allentown. I spent as much time on that street as I did on my own since many of my friends resided there. Houses on Green Street provided a unique perspective to each other due to the steep hill on which they were built. Sitting on Tony's porch, we could see every house clearly, as each one rested a few feet lower than the neighboring house. Next door to Tony lived the Rizzettos, followed by the Sartoris and the Petrafesas. The guys and gals living in those houses were all part of our gang of friends, and we spent hours hanging out on one of their porches in the summer.

During the summer, the families gathered outside in their backyards, sharing conversation. They didn't have to shout from one yard to another to be heard, but most Italians are loud anyway! They shared food from their gardens, cooked out on their grills, and joined one another in a game of cards. A special camaraderie existed with the people of Green Street. Unlike our neighborhood, which was a mix of Germans, Austrians, and Italians, Green Street was almost completely families of Italian descent.

On one occasion, I used our bakery truck to haul my keyboard to Tony's house, and he and I set it up in his back yard. After setting up his drums, Tony and I jammed some tunes, and everyone came out in their back yards and joined in the fun!

Most guys got together in those days for an evening of poker, but our group of guys chose another direction. As bizarre as it may sound, especially when referring to a group of eighteen and nineteen-year-old boys, we gathered at Tony's house on Green Street for games of Monopoly. These were serious, no-holds-barred games! We'd set up in Tony's kitchen right after Tony's mom, Dolly, cleared the dinner table. The game usually began around six in the evening and lasted through the night. Different guys would leave the game and make a food run, returning with cheese steaks, hot dogs, and whatever else had been ordered. We'd take a short break to eat and resume the game. The food break usually came around eight or nine o'clock and was repeated sometime after midnight. Most everyone has played a game of Monopoly at some point and is probably wondering how a game could possibly last all night. The answer is simple, "Deals"! We made deals with each other to stay in the game. One of us might offer three free "landings" on his property in exchange for another's property or building. It was not unheard of for guys to deal in actual dollars to buy their way out of a financial jam! As I said, these were serious games!

We had to vacate Dolly's kitchen in the morning so she could set her table for breakfast, and each guy gathered his "bank" and properties while the board was put away in the closet. No one was permitted access to the board until the following evening. Returning for "night two" with our cash and property cards, we resumed the game. The games usually lasted two nights, with a few stretching into a third night. We truly needed a life! A meeting was held after several of these marathon games, and it was decided that each guy was permitted to make no more than three deals in the game. That cut down the time considerably, not to mention our food budget for late night snack runs!

Although not the most cerebral guys in the neighborhood, we replaced our Monopoly marathons with chess tournaments. Once again, Dolly's kitchen became the venue for these games. We usually played two games simultaneously at each end of the kitchen table. Occasionally, some of the guys would stand around and watch, but they usually only stopped by when it was time for their game to be played. It certainly made Dolly happy to have a smaller crowd in her kitchen!

If we weren't meeting in front of Doc's or my house, we gathered on Tony's front porch before setting out with the girls on an adventure. Gerry Rizzetto had gotten a job at Buddy's Beef-burgers, a long-defunct hamburger stand created to compete with McDonald's. Buddy's was located on Union Boulevard and offered burgers for the amazing price of ten cents. We weren't happy that our friend wasn't able to join us for our summer adventures now that he had become part of the working class, but we certainly didn't mind the perks that came with his new position. Whatever we were doing that night, we drove to Buddy's, and making sure Gerry was our server, we ordered a bag of ten-cent burgers. Gerry stuffed three times as many burgers as we had ordered into our bag and charged us for two or three burgers. That lasted about a week before Gerry was handing us our "special" bag with his boss standing behind him. It was good to have Gerry back with us the next evening. He had become a member of the unemployed!

Gerry was a unique individual! One evening, we were having a party in my parents' basement. Dad gave me the OK, if there was no booze, and I kept the number of people to a minimum. Before Dad and my mom went out for the evening, he made certain to let me know he had complete trust in me, and I wasn't going to let him down. The party was going great until one of the older guys left to go to the I-Club for a drink. When he returned, he brought close to a dozen friends with him. I didn't know any of his friends, and they had all been drinking. I knew my mom and dad would be returning soon and had no idea how to get these people out of my house! I confided in Gerry that I was scared to death and needed help. Within two minutes, Gerry returned from the back room, his arms filled with coats. He proceeded to put coats on the intruders and began pushing them out the door. The fact that the coats he was putting on these people weren't theirs didn't matter to him. When they tried to tell him they were wearing the wrong coat, he told them to "figure it out when they got outside." Five minutes later, the room was empty!

Gerry. He was unique.

Mom and Dad arrived twenty minutes later and stopped down to see how things were going before heading to bed. Dad let me know how pleased he was with the way I handled the responsibility of the party. When he and my mom went upstairs, I gave Gerry a hug. As I said, this guy was unique!

Top: The Green Street Rogue's Gallery.
Above: Our version of The Little Rascals.

28.

Rollie

One of the more colorful characters in our group of guys was, and still is, my dear friend Rollie. He was a shrewd businessman who always seemed to come out on the better end of a deal. Ready to trade army men, I visited him at his house just down the street from mine, carrying five or six of my favorites only to return a half-hour later with one of Rollie's soldiers. Incredibly, I always felt good about the transaction, believing I had made the better deal!

Rollie convinced our group to grab our snow shovels and follow him during a snowy Saturday in January. He had a customer who was willing to pay good money to have her driveway shoveled. Working enthusiastically, we finished the task in less than two hours and headed home. At Rollie's suggestion, I picked up some rolls from my dad's bakery, and we headed to Russoli's market. Did I mention that Rollie's last name is Russoli? After selecting several pounds of Italian lunchmeat, cheese, peppers and tomatoes, Rollie placed our shoveling money into his Dad's cash-regis-

Rollie, my mentor and friend.

ter. Deal complete!

Soon after, we headed to our friend Chas's house where we feasted on some mouth watering Italian cuisine! The sandwiches were amazing, but we couldn't help thinking that, with our money in his dad's register, somehow Rollie had gotten the better of us again.

Rollie owned one of the most unusual automobiles our group had ever seen. It was a white Simca, a small, four-door sedan made in France. Several of us had the privilege of riding to school in it. During my sophomore year in high school, I was one of the lucky people to do so. In addition to gas money which, by the way, I felt was a reasonable request, although I'm certain that car got about two-hundred miles to the gallon, Rollie added a few additional "charges." In the winter, we paid five cents each to run the heater. I was always grateful the Simca didn't have air-conditioning. I don't think I could have afforded it! If it rained, there was a nominal fee for the use of the windshield wipers. When the weather grew milder, we could put the windows down, for a fee, of course. I always managed to absorb these additional fees; however, the charge that took me to the brink of financial ruin was the fee for yelling out the window! I couldn't seem to resist calling out to a friend or a pretty girl, and my itemized bill (yes, Rollie presented each of us a weekly itemized bill) reflected those extra charges.

I believe that the Simca deserves special mention in this story. This strange, little car from Paris appeared to be made of plastic! I realize that every automobile must contain a large portion of steel, but plastic was not lost on this vehicle. Whenever Rollie rounded a curve, those of us in the rear seat leaned to the side, and I'm certain we heard a "cracking" sound. The car was amazingly light, which provided many opportunities for us to lift it and place it somewhere other than its current resting place! Upon leaving a dance with his date, Rollie found his Simca on the top step of the building in which the dance had been held. On another occasion, we set the car in his father's pool at the bungalow. What can I say, it was just too tempting not to pick up that cute, little car and do something with it. When the autumn weather arrived, it was incumbent upon us to bury the entire car with leaves.

One very cold winter night, Rollie, Tony, and I were at Castle Rock. The weather was quite treacherous with a fine glaze of ice coating the roads when we left for home. As Rollie drove through Dorney Park towards the exit, the Simca, light as it was, began to slide in every direction. As we approached a cornfield, plowed over for the winter, Tony suggested that we might make better traction if Rollie left the road and drove through the cornfield. Rollie considered this and decided to give it a try. We bucked and bumped along, and as Rollie shifted the car into second gear, something inside the gearshift snapped. I still say there was an awful lot of plastic in that car! Unable to shift into another gear, Rollie drove the final ten miles home in second gear.

Rollie had an uncanny way with women. A senior, he was far worldlier than I, a lowly sophomore. Experiencing my first crush, I naturally went to him for his advice. It was at that point that he became my mentor in the way of romance. He told me the first thing I needed to do was to call her on the phone and just have a casual conversation with her. Considering I had never said more than "hello" to this girl, the thought of an entire conversation paralyzed me. Knowing this was never going to happen from my home phone unless my entire family moved to Canada for a week, I chose the phone booth at Doc's for this monumental task.

My mentor told me to write down some notes on a piece of paper to avoid a prolonged lull in the conversation. After dropping a dime in the pay phone and dialing the final digit, I knew there was no turning back. Suddenly, all the oxygen was sucked out the door, and the tiny booth seemed to reach a temperature of a hundred degrees! I struggled through a page of the most mundane topics known to man and said, "goodbye," convinced I would never see or hear from this girl for the rest of my life! Surprisingly, my mentor knew his stuff. She was interested! The next part of Rollie's plan was a bit more complicated. It involved our weekly Saturday night trip to Castle Rock. Following the infamous "phone call," I began dancing with this young lady, who was part of the group of girls with whom we hung out.

On the night in question, Rollie arranged to take me and the young lady home. Since the three of us lived within two blocks of each other, it made perfect sense. Rollie told me he would drop both of us at her house, and after seeing her to the door, I could walk home from there. The girl was rather diminutive in stature, so being six feet two inches tall, I was going to have a difficult time kissing her goodnight. Because she lived in an apartment, with several flights of outdoor steps leading to her door, Rollie told me to stop on the stairway until she took two more steps thus equalizing our height difference. This sounded like a great plan, except that she was on a mission to get to the door at the top of the stairs. I walked home that night, still in search of that elusive kiss!

Summer arrived and found our gang of guys and girls on our traditional blanket near the Jordan pool. The girl in question was lying face down sunning herself while everyone else headed for the pool. After taking a few steps toward the pool, I felt a hand on my arm. My mentor looked at me like I had sun-stroke! He told me to lie on the blanket and put my arm around her. I lay down, and fighting a terrible cramp in my arm, reached over and put my arm around her. At that moment, a shrill whistle sounded, and a lifeguard stood over us saying, "None of that!" Seriously?

That first kiss eventually came to pass, and everything worked out for the best. Although not the last, that young lady was certainly the first love of my life!

A few years later, while living in Utah during my time at Utah State University, I wrote a letter to my friend Rollie, who was serving in Vietnam at the time. I also sent him a tiny American flag. Fifty years later, he sent me a message on Facebook. Along with his text, he sent a photo. It was a picture of that American flag that he still has today.

29.

Music's Our Game

During the summer of 1962, Tony approached me with the idea of starting a band. He had begun drum lessons with Tommy Check, an Allentown drum sensation who had placed second in the nation in youth competition at the age of nine and went onto drum with the Jimmy Mulidore Flamingo Hotel Orchestra in Las Vegas. Tony's first set of drums belonged to Tommy Check at one time. He gave them to Tony when Tony began lessons with him. I had been playing keyboard for several years by then, and I thought that maybe Tony had a good idea about a band. We approached a friend of ours by the name of Tom Makoul to see if he had any interest in this venture. Tom liked the idea, although he had no musical experience at the time. Tom was a hustler who worked at his dad's used car dealership, and he quickly went out and purchased a bass guitar, took some lessons, and was all in on our idea.

Tony and I had learned about a guy living in Allentown who was quite good with a guitar, and we went to his apartment to meet him. We introduced ourselves and asked him to play a little something for us. He was more of a chords guy, which he knew well, but what he really had was a voice! The man could flat out sing! He had a gentle, mellow voice that was tailor-made for ballads, and when the band finally formed, and Eddie sang, "Could This Be Magic," the ladies in the crowd swooned!

We were making progress, but we still lacked the main ingredient – a lead guitar player! We found him in a quiet, soft-spoken guy by the name of Skip Mertz. I'm not certain anymore how we found him, but it was the greatest coup for all of us. Skip may have been quiet, but he had a sense of humor that kept all of us in stitches! We had a band! The next thing we needed was a place to rehearse. Tom provided that, at first, by talking his dad into allowing us to use the car dealership after hours. However, the office was cramped and lacked adequate room for our equipment. Tony's dad, Louie, who was a board member at the Italian Club, eventually received permission from the board members to allow us to use the stage in the large banquet room. We were even allowed to store our equipment there between rehearsals. It was a perfect venue for us! We had a stage and a large room that provided excellent acoustics. We met at the I-Club every night after dinner for two or three hours of rehearsal.

As autumn gave way to winter, we had become a real band, complete with a repertoire of songs, popular at the time, and we were getting close to taking that next step of acquiring jobs in local clubs and bars; however, there was still a matter that needed to be addressed. We had no name for the band! Tom, who ironically had the least amount of musical ability, took over as our leader. As I said earlier, he was a hustler! Tom's idea was to approach the owner of one of our leading men's stores in Allentown and use the store's name. In exchange for the "free advertising" Tom told the owner that all he needed to do was supply us with clothing from his store. Although it sounded reasonable to us, the store owner nixed the idea, but that couldn't prevent us from adopting the name of the store as our band's name. The Gentrys were born, and the owner of Gentry's clothing store didn't seem to mind. Tom had a thousand business cards printed with our contact information, and the slogan on the card read, "Music's Our Game, The Gentrys, Our Name."

Members of today's bands show up for their gig dressed in everything from jeans to sweatpants, but in the sixties, we wanted to project an image of class. Although we were unable to make a deal with Gentrys men store, we decided to shop together for outfits. We wore powder-blue blazers on certain occasions, as well as black blazers with gray slacks for other jobs. We looked good, and I always felt it was important to our clients.

Tony jams with me on the front porch.

The first gig of our career came on the unlikely night of New Year's Eve. We made some calls and were booked at the Emmaus Fire Club. We met with the board members a few days before New Year's Eve, and I was a bit surprised that they wouldn't want us to audition. I realized we weren't booked into Studio 54, but I thought these guys were taking a heck of a risk, booking a band for New

Year's Eve without hearing us perform one song! We rented powder-blue tuxedos for the occasion, and I must say, if nothing else, we looked damned good! The evening turned out to be a rousing success, and several of the patrons asked for one of our business cards. We were on our way!

Our next job came when someone from a fraternity house contacted Tom to play at their party which was held in an old dance hall located in Allentown's defunct Central Park. It was a raucous affair filled with college kids, and we suspected there might have been high school kids there as well. That was not a problem; however, while the band was setting up, we noticed at least a dozen kegs of beer carted in by some of the fraternity brothers. About an hour into the gig, the place was raided! Police entered the building from every available door, and as we played, kids were climbing out windows. While the police were questioning some of the fraternity brothers, Tom made a phone call to his uncle, who happened to be the district attorney at the time. He arrived on the scene as the local police were citing the guys. His presence didn't help them from receiving citations, but he did allow the party to continue. The DA told the police to confiscate every keg and replace them with kegs of root beer! Within twenty minutes, the place was empty! One of the funnier things I remember about the incident was the story in next day's newspaper. It read in part that "the police were having difficulty questioning the students because the band was playing too loud to be heard!"

Another phenomenal lead guitar player from the Allentown area at that time was a guy by the name of Danny Fredericks. Although his style differed from that of Skip Mertz, our lead guitar, he was Skip's equal in every way. For a few brief months, the Gentrys had the privilege of having both these amazing musicians in our band at the same time! Danny was between bands at the time and asked to join us until another job opened. I'm not sure if there was a better band in the valley during those few months. Several nights when we were performing, the two of them got together while we were on break and play "Malaguena" on their acoustical guitars. I was mesmerized by these two guys as were the rest of the club patrons! I always equated having both playing lead guitar in our band was like a Major League Baseball team signing the top two free agents to contracts!

After Danny left the band, the Gentrys grew by one more when Tony's cousin, Chuck, joined the band. Chuck played the sax, and added a new dimension to our sound. We were scheduled to play a winter dance at a high school in Center Valley called Southern Lehigh. I had never heard of the school, and got lost trying to find it. Ironically, years later, I began teaching in that school district and remained there for thirty-six years! However, that night, I couldn't find the darn place! Eventually, I arrived in time, and an hour into the first set, Chuck walked into the gym, playing his sax while we were performing a song on stage. The kids went wild and gathered around him as he walked to the stage. That was Tony's cousin. If Skip were the quiet, low-keyed member of our group, Chuck was the gregarious one!

The Gentrys' popularity grew, and we won several Battle of the Bands events. We were booked in clubs all over the valley and beyond. During the summer of 1963, the Gentry's had an offer for a job at a nightclub named The Alibi in Atlantic City. Unlike the Emmaus Fire Company, the owners of the Alibi insisted we drive to Atlantic City for an audition. The job was to last the entire summer with our playing every night until two a.m. I can't recall for certain, but there may have been a free night during the week. The gig also included a jam-session every Sunday afternoon. I was about to enter my senior year of high school in the fall, and I felt like this was a golden opportunity to enjoy this experience before heading back to school. I was the youngest member of the band

and the only one still in school.

Tony's dad was not thrilled with the idea. Louie was a wonderful man whom I adored as much as my own father, and I know he loved Tony dearly. In his view, this was not a good place for his son at that time, and I respected him for his belief. I know that he had called my dad and was a little disappointed in him that he was going to allow me to go, but he stood his ground with Tony, and that was cool with us. Tony told us to do the audition with a substitute drummer, and if we got the job, he would figure something out with his dad. That concerned all of us because we didn't want bad feelings to come between Tony and his dad. That said, we drove to Atlantic City and took the audition.

The guy that sat in for Tony was a good drummer, but he wasn't Tony, and I think we were off a bit that day. It didn't seem to concern the owner of the Alibi. He told us the job was ours, if we wanted it. Tom told him we would get back to him by the end of the day. As we drove back to Allentown, we had a long talk in the car and decided we didn't want to cause trouble for Tony, and we weren't going to do the job without him. We knew we were going to get plenty of work back home, and quite frankly, I was a bit relieved because taking the job meant I would have to forego my senior year on the football team. I had played football with those guys since eighth grade, and I didn't want to lose my final year. I never offered that feeling to anyone in the band because I didn't want them to view me as some school kid who didn't want to miss his friends!

We ended up taking a job in Easton that Fall, and it really affected my senior year of football and schoolwork. The job began at ten p.m. and lasted until two in the morning. It was a seedy club with many shady characters frequenting the place every night. We never saw the people who owned the club until sometime in the middle of the week when a very large man came up to the stage one night while we were busy packing our equipment. He told us the boss wanted to see us upstairs. We all went up together, and I was certain that every one of us was a bit nervous when we walked into the office. A man, who we decided had to be the owner of the club, told us he was terminating our services. I don't think I was the only band member to feel relieved. It was then that Tom spoke up, and the blood froze in my veins! He told the guy that was fine with the band, but we had a contract with him and expected to be paid for the entire week.

The next thing we knew, the other men in the room crowded around us, staring us down, and the owner said that was not going to happen. Words were exchanged, when Eddie, our mild-mannered crooner, looked one of the guys in the eyes and said, "What you need is a bullet to the head"! At that moment, English class and football practice no longer seemed very important to me. The gentleman who was the recipient of Eddie's comment casually pulled his sport coat back just far enough to reveal a shoulder holster. The man was packing heat!

We departed the club, thankful for the three day's pay we received, but Tom wasn't about to let it go. He contacted the musician's union, of which we were all members in good standing, and a week later, Tom received a check for the four remaining nights. Who said musicians aren't tough? I still remember my coach stopping me in the hall and telling me that I couldn't keep up these late hours and expect to perform well in the classroom or the football field. I told him it was no longer a problem. Our gig with the Easton nightclub was over.

Our final brush with danger, although I don't really think we were in any trouble, came a few weeks later. We had just finished playing a gig at Henry's Hideaway in Center Valley. We had one night left on the job, and we headed to a diner for a late snack before returning home. The next morning the headline in the local paper read, "Local Night-Club Owner Shot Dead." Sometime after we said "goodnight" to the owner of Henry's Hideaway, he was murdered in his club. I began to wonder if this was the path I really wanted to pursue!

Shortly after the new year, an event occurred in February of 1964 that was to change the face of music forever! February 7, 1964 was the day the Beatles landed in America, and nothing was ever the same again. The Gentrys decided to put a Beatles segment into our shows, and we headed to Philadelphia for wigs and suits. We went to a men's store on Broad Street and found gold, sharkskin suits with black velvet lapels, like the suits worn by the Beatles during one of their shows. Unfortunately, I was unable to find a suit in my size. The store-keeper said he had a gold sharkskin suit without the black velvet lapels, and knowing I lived with an amazing seamstress, I bought the suit. From there, we headed to a wig salon and were fitted with perfect Beatle wigs. My mom didn't fail me. She got black velvet and sewed it onto the lapels, and no one could tell the difference between my suit and those worn by the rest of the group.

A few extra rehearsals were needed to nail down enough Beatles songs to fill a set, and we were ready to try them out in public. Our next gig was a fraternity party in Allentown, and after our second set, we went into a dressing room, changed into our suits, donned our wigs and walked out to the stage. The place went wild! During the set, one of the fraternity brothers called the newspaper, and before we ended the set, a photographer and reporter arrived in time to take a picture. The picture appeared in the next day's paper along with an article about the Gentrys. We should have given that fraternity brother a commission, because that photo and article brought us tons of jobs! A week later, we were performing at the Italian Club on a Sunday night. It was a special night for us because many friends and family from our neighborhood were there to see us. What we weren't aware of was that several of the local high schools were sponsoring exchange students from England and Germany, and members of the Board of Allentown Schools brought these students to the Italian Club to hear the Gentrys and see their Beatles Act. One of the girls was an exchange student at my high school, and it was very cool to see her sitting at a table at the club watching our show.

Later that month, we had a gig in Lansford, Pa. Lansford was a small town in the coal regions of Pennsylvania and home to our sax-player. Snow was predicted as we drove north to Lansford for a Saturday show at the Lansford Am-vets. As we were getting ready for our first set, I had a major malfunction with my keyboard. I'm not certain what went wrong, but smoke began to seep out through the keys, and I heard a sound I had never heard before. With our first set minutes away, my keyboard and I were dead in the water! Having no recourse but to sit out the show, I joined a table of young ladies and enjoyed the next three hours having a few beers (yes, I was underage, but this was Lansford!) and dancing with the gals while the Gentrys did their thing. I found it interesting to watch our guys from a patron's perspective. They were very good. The only thing they needed was a fine keyboard player!

We spent the night at Chuck's mom's house and had a delightful time. The snow began falling sometime around midnight, and by morning the ground was covered with four or five inches of fresh snow. This was time for us to make our move, get on the road, and head to Allentown before the weather got any worse. There was a minor problem with that idea. One of the bars in town was sponsoring an afternoon jam session, and Lansford had no intention of cancelling it due to a foot or two of snow! We headed to the club and spent the next three hours listening to music and dancing. When the festivities ended, we headed outside to a winter wonderland! We weren't going anywhere. I called my dad and told him we would be spending Sunday night in Lansford, and I would

Music was our game.

BEATLES AT BERG—Beatlemania came to a Muhlenberg College fraternity house, Lamda Chi Alpha, Saturday. Beneath those wigs are members of the local Gentrys combo, left to right, Chuck Hanna, Ski Mertz, Eddie Kirk, Tony Spagn letti, Turk Makul and Randy Duric The frat party was reported screaming success.

head home on Monday morning. Dad reminded me that Monday was a school day, and I told him I didn't want to risk damaging the car or myself by trying to drive home in this weather. When he asked why I didn't get on the road as soon as I awoke on Sunday, I told him I was having difficulty hearing him because of the bad connection caused by the snow. Monday arrived, and the Gentrys were going nowhere. The good news was that schools in Allentown were closed, so I wasn't missing any class-time.

The storm turned out to be one of the worst blizzards in the last twenty-five years. We spent the entire week snowed in with Chuck's mom and her very small home. Out of food and wearing only the clothing on our backs, we dug into Chuck's closet and selected everything from underwear and socks to pants, shirts, sweaters...anything we could find. We set out by foot to find an open market, finally finding a small grocery store. Using money from the job, we stocked Chuck's mom's house and slept on the floor. Allentown's schools closed for the entire week, so Mom and Dad weren't too upset with my winter vacation.

One very late evening, I was returning from a job in Bethlehem. It was almost three o'clock in the morning, and I had just turned onto Jordan Street from Tilghman Street and was only three blocks from home. I looked to my right and saw my neighbor, Joe, sitting on the steps of Palladino's Cafe. Joe was a nice man, but he weighed well over four hundred pounds. I knew it would take Joe until daylight to walk those three blocks from the cafe to his home, and I also knew he was not in very good health. I was exhausted, but I had to stop the car and ask him if he wanted a ride home. He was grateful for the ride, and I knew getting him in my car wasn't going to be easy. Anytime the Gentrys had a gig, I removed the rear seat from my ‘56 Chevy to fit my keyboard in the back. Because of this, I could move my seat far back from the steering wheel. I did just that, and I was barely able to reach the gas pedal or brake with my foot, but there was no other way Joe was going to fit in my car. It took about ten minutes, but together we got Joe into the passenger seat. I drove the three blocks to my house, helped Joe out of the passenger seat and up the three steps to his house. By now, the final three blocks between me and a peaceful night's rest had taken well over an hour!

Eventually, the back seat of my '56 Chevy was no longer suitable for my keyboard. I had replaced my smaller keyboard with a Hammond B-3. It was the instrument being used by most keyboard players during that time. Along with the Hammond came a Leslie speaker, which was about the size of a small refrigerator! While the other guys were packing up guitars and amps and throwing them in their trunks, I was using my dad's bakery truck to haul a few hundred pounds of keyboard and speaker to every job! The B-3, like most Hammonds at the time, weren't filled with transistors, but rather tubes, and their cabinets were made of solid wood. On one occasion, we had a wedding reception gig on the second floor of a hotel. When we arrived, and asked the proprietor where the elevator was, we were told there wasn't any. It took all five Gentrys to get that keyboard up the stairs. I don't know if I was ever going to get anywhere with my music, but playing in that band certainly kept my muscles well-toned!

During the summer of '64, the Gentrys hired a record technician to come to the I-Club for one of our rehearsals. He and his assistant used his supply of switchboards, mixers and recording equipment to cut a demo tape for us. A few days later, Tom set up an appointment with Parkway Studios in Philadelphia, and the five of us headed to Philly for a meeting. To our surprise, the man liked our sound and told us he would like to set up a recording session at the end of summer, most likely in late September. We were excited about the prospect of returning to Philly in the fall, but that session never materialized. In August, Eddie, our smooth-voiced crooner, departed for Nashville where he became a studio musician. Skip opened a bicycle shop, while Tony and Tom opened a teenage nightclub called the Mad Hatter on the southside of Allentown. I left for Utah, and just like that, the Gentrys were no more. There were only a few copies of that demo record produced. I had one of the copies. Unfortunately, I left it in the rear of my '56 Chevy while I was at the shore. With all the windows closed and the temperature in the low nineties, the record curled up like a potato chip! Years later, one of the students in my eighth-grade English class told me that her aunt used to follow our band whenever we were playing, and she had a copy of our demo record. How she came into possession of it, I'll never know. At any rate, I offered to pay her aunt fifty dollars for the record. She refused my offer.

30.

The Ghost of '64

The year was 1964. My friends and I had grown up with our beloved Phillies, watching them on TV, listening to every game on the radio, and making an occasional trip to Philadelphia to see a ball game. Many of the older men in our neighborhood were still Yankees fans. Italian Americans like Joe DiMaggio, Phil Rizzuto and Yogi Berra certainly had an influence on the men who frequented the Italian Club to watch the Bronx Bombers play on TV. The Phillies were no "Bombers" in any sense of the word. They were usually mired in, or near, the bottom of the National League during every year of my childhood; however, this year was different. This year was 1964, and the Phillies were leading the National League by six and a half games with only twelve games remaining on the schedule. There were no divisions in the Major Leagues in those days, and the words "Wild Card" only pertained to poker. There was a National League and an American League. Two league champions who met in the World Series to determine the best team in baseball!

In early June, my friends and I were enjoying a beautiful afternoon at Lehigh Parkway, socializing with the girls and listening to our radios. Tony turned his car radio to the Phillies game to check on our boys. It was Father's Day, and Jim Bunning was on the bump for the Phils. Byrum Saam had just announced that Bunning was still pitching a perfect game after five innings! With that news, we hopped in Tony's car and drove back to his house. When we arrived, Louie, Tony's dad, already had the game on TV, and we all gathered around the set to watch history! When Bunning struck out Mets pinch-hitter, John Stevenson, to end the game, the stadium erupted, as did the guys watching from Tony's house. This was going to be the year!

It was a chilly Tuesday evening on September 21, when Dad and I began the first mix of dough at our bakery. We normally didn't work a night shift at the bakery and had already worked earlier that day to get Tuesday's bread out to the stores and restaurants. New York was the host of the World's Fair that year, and none of us had ever gone to a World's Fair before. Wednesday was to be the day that changed. To make that happen, however, Dad had to make sure everyone received delivery of our bread that day. Since the only two people who worked in the bakery were Dad and I, there was no one to prepare Wednesday's bread for delivery. We were both going to the fair along with my mom, sister, brother, and my girlfriend, who skipped a day of college classes to make the trip. Dad and I prepared the orders and packaged them for the guys to deliver the bread the following morning.

The Phillies were beginning a home-stand at Connie Mack Stadium, and having the game on the radio made that evening's second shift of work a little easier to bear. Listening as we worked, Dad and I breezed through Tuesday night's task. The Phillies were six and a half games up, and with only twelve games remaining, and only needed to win a few more to lock up the pennant. As Dad and I continued to fashion loaves of bread, Art Mahaffey, the Phillies fire-baller continued to mow down the Cincinnati Reds, and the game remained scoreless for five innings. In the top of the sixth inning, Chico Ruiz, a Reds utility player, entered the game and singled off Mahaffey. Ruiz was a flake, who rarely played, and sat in the dugout wearing alligator baseball shoes while perched on his personal rubber seat cushion with an electric fan to keep him cool.

With two outs, Ruiz had reached third base with the dangerous, future Hall of Famer Frank Robinson coming to the plate. Logic would dictate Chico to hang close to the bag and wait for Robinson to drive him in, but there was nothing logical about Chico Ruiz! With Robinson digging in, Mahaffey began his long, high wind-up, and Ruiz broke for home. His manager never gave him a sign to steal, and he was on his own. That was Chico. He truly was a flake! Not on this night, however. Ruiz slid into home for the only run of the game, and the Phillies had lost a heart-breaker, 1-0. Not a big deal at the time, but it was the beginning of ten days of horror for me and every kid in our neighborhood. The Saint Louis Cardinals were six and a half games behind the Phillies at the beginning of Tuesday's night's game, but after winning their game that night, had moved to within five and a half games. Not to worry.

The next day, the entire family took a bus, sponsored by the Italian Club, to Flushing Meadows, site of the New York World's Fair, and I didn't give one thought to last night's 1-0 defeat at the hands of the Reds. It was a beautiful afternoon, and we thoroughly enjoyed the fair. I arrived home after a wonderful day in time to watch the final few innings of the Phillies game, a 9-2 defeat at the hands of the Reds. Gene Mauch, the Phillies manager, then did something totally amazing to me and my friends, not to mention the citizens of Philadelphia. Mauch began pitching his two aces, Jim Bunning and Chris Short, on two days' rest. This did nothing to halt the downward spiral. Following another loss to the Reds, the Phils were swept by the Milwaukee Braves and Saint Louis Cardinals. I would like to say that being eighteen years old by this time I was handling this well, but truth be told, I began crawling out of bed after each devastating game, putting my clothing back on, and walking the streets! Some nights, I walked until midnight, unable to sleep. My friends and I had waited our entire young lives for this moment, and it seemed to be quickly slipping through our fingers!

The streak stretched to ten games, and by the time it ended, the Phillies, who had been in first place all season long, had fallen to third place. My brother had gone to a game at the stadium prior to the beginning of the streak and had purchased a pennant stating, "Philadelphia Phillies, National League Champions"! It, of course, was dated 1964. He still has that pennant, fastened to the wall behind his bar - definitely a collector's item!

All was not lost; however. The Phillies had two games remaining with the Cincinnati Reds. If they could win them both, and the Saint Louis Cardinals, now in first place, lost their last three games against the awful New York Mets, the Phils would tie Saint Louis and force a playoff. The baseball gods seem to step in as the Phillies ended their losing streak and won their last two games against the Reds, the final game, a 10-0 thrashing of Cincinnati! Meanwhile, the Mets, who were called the worst team he ever saw by their manager, Casey Stengel, defeated the Saint Louis Cardinals two days in a row!

Holding on to the slimmest hope, the guys gave me money, and I began driving to Philadelphia. There were no such things as online orders in those days, and my mission was to arrive in Philadelphia at the end of the Mets-Cardinals game, hopefully a Mets victory, in time to buy tickets for the playoff game. Listening to the game on my radio as I drove, I was encouraged by the fact that the lowly Mets were beating Saint Louis 3-2 in the fifth inning. About fifteen miles farther down the Pennsylvania Turnpike, I searched for the nearest exit. The Cardinals stormed back to win the game 11-5. The dream had ended. It would take an additional sixteen years before our beloved Phillies won the National League pennant and went on to win their first World Series.

I sure did enjoy the World's Fair!

31.

Pipe Dream

One of the most difficult decisions I had to make in my young life began with a talk I had with my dad at the beginning of summer. I told him that I needed to find a job to take care of myself. I didn't want to rely on Mom and Dad to support me forever. That meant not working with my dad in the bakery that summer. The decision was made easier because Mom had retired from her hostess job at the motor lodge, and I knew he wouldn't be alone. Dad was fine with my decision, as I knew he would be. That was the kind of man he was!

I took a job with Buckeye Pipeline, a company located in Macungie, Pa., and was told to report to a town west of Fogelsville, where I would be met by an official from Buckeye. The town is so small, I cannot recall its name. I was to meet this person at eight a.m. in the middle of a farmer's field, and as I drove down the narrow, dirt road leading to the meeting place, I wondered what I had gotten myself into. The field belonged to a local farmer who had leased the property to Buckeye because of its proximity to a set of railroad tracks. When I arrived, I noticed that there were already men working in the field, and I found the supervisor from Buckeye waiting to greet me.

He explained to me that Buckeye was running a pipeline of natural gas through the state, and what I was seeing in the field was a temporary pipe yard. Freight cars loaded with enormous steel pipes, approximately sixty feet long and weighing over a thousand pounds, were unloaded at this yard. A large crane sat in the yard awaiting the arrival of the cars. Two men were stationed on top of the freight car, and it was their job to attach the two cables, extending from the crane, to each end of the pipe. The crane then lifted the pipe into the yard and set it on the skids. More men then rolled the pipe down the skids and set it in place at the rear of the stack. Pipes were stored here, awaiting trucks to enter the yard at which time, using the crane, pipes would be loaded onto the trucks for delivery to the right-of-way.

The Buckeye supervisor informed me that the people in the pipe yard, including the crane operator and truckers, were independent contractors, not affiliated with Buckeye. My job, as an employee of Buckeye, was to record the serial number of each freight car, the number of pipes on the car, and measure the length of each pipe. All this information would be recorded in a log book and signed by me. I had already been given a list of serial numbers of the freight cars that were supposed to arrive that day, and it was my job to make sure my list of numbers matched the numbers given to me by Buckeye.

Eventually, I had the opportunity to see where the pipes ended up. The right-of-way contained miles of channel dug into the earth where the pipe would lay. The pipes were unloaded, end to end next to the channel, and welders were brought in to connect them. The pipes were beveled at the ends where the weld was to be placed. Before the pipe, now one long, rope-like section, was snaked into the channel, inspectors brought in x-ray equipment and x-rayed every weld. If a weld was not perfect, the welder was fired. It seemed heartless to me to fire these guys for one bad weld, but the supervisor explained to me that the pipe was going to be carrying natural gas under sixteen-hundred pounds of pressure, and every weld had to be perfect!

My first day in the yard proved to be an inauspicious one. My log showed one less freight car than Buckeye had listed on its records for that day. My supervisor came to the yard near the end of the day and gave me a stern reprimand for losing track of a freight car on my first day. I was mystified. Certain I had not missed recording any freight car on that first day, I drove to the railroad office the following morning before reporting to the pipe yard and spoke with the station master. After explaining my dilemma to the man, I waited as he made a few phone calls and checked his records. The missing car was found! It had ended up in Canada by mistake.

Vindicated, I headed to the pipe yard. The station master had already contacted Buckeye, and my supervisor showed up a half hour later to apologize. He added that I had done a good job of locating the missing car. That night, my dad, after listening to my account of the entire incident, shook my hand and told me he was proud of me. There aren't many things a son can hear from his father that mean more to him than that!

As time passed, I got to know the men in the pipe yard. I was the "kid" in their eyes, with the soft job. They teased me about my "easy living," but it was good-natured kidding. These guys were from Scranton, Pa. That was coal country, filled with some pretty tough characters! That said, I enjoyed these men, and I had no problem "dishing" it right back to them! It was bloody hot that first week, and I showed up for work in shorts and a T-shirt, knowing these guys were going to give me the business. They referred to me as "Beach Boy" and told me to put some clothes on before I burned to a crisp. I told them they were just too old to handle the sun and very soft for guys from Scranton! A few nights later, I couldn't sleep. The back of my neck was on fire with sunburn. When I arrived at the pipe yard wearing a cowboy hat and a wet towel draped over my neck, the Scranton men began singing one of the Beach Boys songs while dancing around the yard. I must admit, it was hilarious!

After a few weeks, I had the recording stuff down pat. I could log all the cars and record the length of each pipe by the middle of the day. I went to the foreman of the yard and asked him if I could help in the yard. These guys were not union, and I wasn't going to be stealing anyone's job. The foreman told me I wasn't required to work for the contractors, and I shouldn't allow his men to intimidate me into working in the yard. I let him know it was my decision to work, and I didn't feel any pressure from the guys in the yard. He agreed to let me work in the yard provided I completed my work for Buckeye. He didn't want any problems with them. Having watched these guys for several weeks, I knew what to do, and I joined in unloading pipes onto the skids and loading the trucks when they entered the yard. As we were loading pipes onto one of the trucks, I made the mistake of standing with my back against the cab of the truck. As the pipe swung into the truck, the pipe pinned me against the truck cab. I felt a crushing pressure against my chest and was unable to breathe. The crane operator saw what had happened and quickly backed the crane off. The guys pulled the pipe back, and I was free to slide off the truck. I fell to the ground, gasping for air. A perfect ring marked my chest for the rest of the week.

The next day I arrived at the yard expecting the cold shoulder. I figured the guys would be disgusted with the "dumb" kid who had no business working in the yard. I was wrong. Those tough men from coal country couldn't have been nicer. They checked with me every day, asking how I was feeling and offering advice to make sure I didn't get caught in that situation again.

We had been working five eight-hour days; however, bad weather had caused delays in the pipe-line, and an extra day was added to the work week. With more bad weather taking its toll on the project, our hours were upgraded to ten, and we were now working six ten-hour days a week! The line had moved far enough past our present location, and it was time to move the pipe yard to a new location. We spent the day tearing down the skids and loading them onto a truck before traveling to Aquashicola, Pa., a small down north of Palmerton where we set up a new yard in another lot leased by Buckeye. The Buckeye supervisor reminded me once again that I was "not required" to tear down or load skids, but I was enjoying the work. Once the new yard was in place and pipes began filling the skids, my supervisor asked me if I would like to leave the yard for a few days to help him on the right-of-way. I thought the experience would be interesting, so a substitute was brought in to keep my log book at the yard while I headed out on the road with my boss. The pipeline was nearing the Blue Mountains of Pennsylvania, and would soon be crossing over the mountains. There were private homes and businesses in the mountains that Buckeye needed to address to pass through their property. Most of the time, the work was routine. We talked to the resident, signed a contract, and moved on to the next location. One morning, we arrived at a house on the side of the mountain that appeared run down and a little ominous from the outside. My supervisor knocked on the door, and it swung open with a crash. The man standing in front of us was holding a shotgun aimed directly at our chests! My entire body froze, as the man told us to get the hell off his property! As soon as I could get my feet to move, that's exactly what we did. I'll never know if that shotgun was loaded or not, but I was glad to be back in my boss's car. It wasn't clear to me if Buckeye worked something out with that man or chose to move the right-of-way, but the pipeline continued to climb the Blue Mountains of Pennsylvania.

Not sorry to leave right-of-way work behind me, I was given the opportunity to remain outside the yard a little while longer and join a boring crew. No, this was not a crew that bored people, but rather a group of men responsible for boring holes under streets and highways for the pipes to pass through. It was interesting work, and I remember boring a channel under the Pennsylvania Turnpike at one point in our work. Every so often, we would hit rock under the road, and that required the use of dynamite to break up the rock before continuing to bore the channel. A stick of dynamite was attached to a long pole and placed into the channel until it reached the bed of rock. The fuse was lit, and we scattered behind the trucks awaiting the blast.

One afternoon, we were boring under a rural road somewhere north of Aquashicola when we struck a bed of stone. We had been working on that road for most of the day and hadn't seen a single vehicle the entire time. As the men readied the dynamite, one of the guys asked the foreman if he wanted him to walk up the road and flag down any vehicle before we blasted. The foreman told him, "There hasn't been a vehicle on this road all day. Let's just blow this thing and get it over with." As the foreman lit the fuse and we began to scatter, a delivery van came into view. Apparently, he was lost, and he stopped a few feet from the channel and stepped out of his truck to ask us for directions. The foreman leaped out from behind his truck and ran towards the man. Hearing the foreman shout to him to get back in his truck and back the hell out of there, the driver climbed into his van and started it just as the dynamite exploded. All four wheels of the van lifted a few inches off the road, and the shaken man took off in the opposite direction never to be seen again!

As much as I enjoyed the experience working on the right-of-way, I was glad to return to the yard. It was good to see the men from Scranton again, and returning to my log book, I began checking the railroad cars as they came into the yard. Every crane had two men in charge of its operation. There was the operator of the crane, responsible for hoisting the pipes from the freight cars, and the oiler. The oiler's job was to load the crane onto the truck bed and drive it to the next yard. Another responsibility of the oiler was to make sure the crane was well-oiled and greased. A heavy-duty grease gun lay on the bed of the crane during each work day. One afternoon, I decided to have a little fun with the Scranton boys. I discovered that, by pumping the handle on the grease gun sharply, I could shoot a glob of grease out of the gun. The glob could travel twenty feet if I pumped the handle down hard enough. It was nearing the end of August, and temperatures had climbed into the nineties. I began "shooting" globs of grease at the men stationed on the freight car. Most of the time, the globs flew innocently past them, but occasionally, one would smack them in the chest. Unable to leave their position on the freight car, the men were at my mercy! This went on for an hour, and the Scranton boys were unhappy with the "kid." The "Beach Boy" had them pretty sore!

Aquashicola had a bar! I think it was the only bar in the entire town. During my lunch break, I went into the bar, ordered a soft drink, and took my lunch down to a small clearing near the creek that ran past the yard. It was a peaceful spot, and a great place to enjoy my lunch and relax against a tree until it was time for work. I was sitting against a tree, almost fast asleep, when a bunch of hands grabbed me from both sides and pulled me against the tree. While two of the Scranton boys held me, another tied me to the tree. I knew what was coming! The three of them, hands loaded with grease, proceeded to rub it in my hair, on my clothes, and on my face! Before heading back to the yard, they loosened the rope, and I freed myself. When I returned to the pipe yard, everyone was working. Everything came to a halt for a few minutes as the men from Scranton cheered and laughed hysterically! We had a long, hot afternoon of work ahead of us, and as the day wore on, I began to smell terrible. I tried to clean as much grease from my hair and clothing before getting into my car for the long drive back to Allentown, but by the time I arrived at the house, my Ford Falcon smelled like a grease pit from the local garage!

As the dog-days of summer wore on, more bad weather meant longer hours. Our work week was upgraded to seven ten-hour days, and I was beginning to forget what day of the week it was. On a rainy day, for which I was extremely grateful, I met my good friend, Chas DeFanti, for lunch at a local diner. The conversation that took place during our lunch had a profound effect on my life. It was that conversation that changed my future!

32.

Follow That Blonde

I loved my job with Buckeye, and the people with whom I worked became a treasured part of my life. The pipeline was moving closer to the hometown of the Scranton guys and farther from my home every day. Seven ten-hour days is a long, grueling stretch, even for a job that I enjoyed. My friend, Chas DeFanti, was iron-working at the time, and in addition to his long hours, the work was dangerous. Chas and I met for lunch at a diner in Allentown, and while we were waiting for our food, Chas said to me, "Do we really want to do this for the rest of our lives?" "Do we want to climb on steel girders every day?" "How long do you want to work seventy hours a week with no life of which to speak?" I was taken aback by his questions, and I said to him, "What can we do about it?" Chas said we needed to go to college and make our lives better! After a promising beginning to my education, my scholastic career had taken a nose dive, and I couldn't see a way clear to the path Chas had outlined.

We decided, at that moment, to make it happen, and by the time the check arrived, Chas and I were on a mission! Our first move was to contact Moravian College in Bethlehem and enroll in several classes. In addition to an English class, which I loved, we chose to take Algebra II. As I mentioned earlier in this book, it was algebra that brought my scholastic career to a crashing halt. If I didn't have any success with Algebra I, how was I going to handle the sequel? In addition to those two courses, we also chose to take psychology.

I think I was going to need the psychology course, if I were going to have any chance to pass Algebra II! Mom and Dad were amazed with my endeavor, and I made sure that I paid for the classes with money I earned on the pipeline.

During the semester of work, our English professor called me into his office. He told me that I had an excellent grasp of English and my answers to his essay questions showed a great deal of promise. There was still that little matter of Algebra II. Chas and I studied together, and he was much stronger in that area than I. If I were going to pay this money and take this leap, I had to make it work. Not only did I ace the algebra final, but I received an A for the course! My sister, Anita, who was in college at the time, was astounded when I shared the news with her. She had worn herself out trying to tutor me in Algebra I, years earlier.

Chas. Our conversation changed my life.

While we were taking the courses at Moravian, Chas and I met other people with situations like ours. They, too, were looking for something better for themselves. I spoke with one of the students in our psychology class during a break, and he showed me a brochure he had received in the mail from Utah State University. I asked him if I could borrow it for the evening to look it over. Chas and I had decided, and we had taken the first step by signing up for these classes, but it was time to get moving on the real reason we were doing all of this.

We began considering colleges, and at one point he and I, along with another student, traveled to some of the local colleges and universities.

I really liked what I read in the Utah brochure and suggested to Chas he might be interested in looking at it, but he decided to apply to Indiana University of Pennsylvania. I decided to send my Moravian transcript to Utah State and roll the dice! Two weeks passed, and having left the pipeline job to take the Moravian classes, I was working with my dad in the bakery. Returning from the shop one afternoon, I found a letter from Utah State informing me that I had been accepted. Chas had been accepted to Indiana University, and we were both on our way.

I knew very little about the protocol for entering college. I've watched young kids, including my own, attend orientation days at school, often with their parents, where they were given schedules, information about their dormitories, and other important details necessary for a smooth transition from high school to college. None of this was going to happen in my case. The day was gray and rainy as I boarded an airplane in Allentown. Dad was already into his first mix at the bakery, so it was just Mom, Sis, and my girlfriend there to see me off on this new adventure. I had never flown before, and I remember climbing the steps of the propeller-driven plane from the tarmac. There were no enclosed tunnels to pass through as we do today. I was off! After a stop in Chicago's O'Hare Airport, I boarded my first jet plane and headed to Salt Lake City. I remember the plane being virtually empty, and a stewardess approaching me during the beginning of the flight. To all the flight attendants, who might resent the term "stewardess" I apologize, but that was the term used at the time! The stewardess told me to follow her to the first-class section of the plane. She said the flight was "empty," and it was OK for me to sit there. Sipping champagne and eating macadamia nuts all the way to Utah, I thought to myself that this air travel stuff wasn't too bad!

The plane arrived in Salt Lake City around one in the afternoon, and lugging two suitcases (no wheels!) I walked to the local bus station. I bought a ticket to Logan, Utah, which was eighty miles north of Salt Lake City, and asked the clerk when the bus to Logan was leaving. I was told it would depart Salt Lake City at eleven p.m.! Remember when I said I was leaving Allentown on my new "adventure"? The adventure was just beginning! Sitting in the bus terminal, I began thinking about what I was going to do when I arrived in Logan around two o'clock in the morning. I found a phone book and looked up Utah State University. Searching the various departments, I found one listed as "housing" with the name of the housing director behind it. His name was Mr. Oswald. I will never forget his name, although I'm certain he has done his level best to forget mine!

I called the number and asked to speak with Mr. Oswald. I told him my name, as if that would mean something to him, and said I was arriving in Logan at two in the morning and would need a place to sleep. He asked me the name of the dormitory listed on my orientation papers, and seemed genuinely surprised when I told him I had no such papers. He told me he would meet me at the bus station in Logan when the bus arrived. It had been one very long day, and as I stepped off the bus in Logan just before two o'clock, I saw a man wearing his pajamas, slippers, and an overcoat. It could only be Mr. Oswald. I walked over to him and introduced myself. As he stared at me through eyes glazed over from sleep, he said to me, "Grab your bags and follow me." OK, the man wasn't overjoyed to see me, but who could blame him?

Throwing my suitcases into the bed of his pick-up, he told me to hop in, and we drove off. We rode in silence for about forty minutes, passing stark prairie, framed by massive mountains, their moonlit peaks topped with a September snow, before arriving at a set of buildings. Mr. Oswald pulled into a parking space near one of the buildings and handed me a key. He told me to go to unit 34-C (some things one never forgets!). After unloading my suitcases from the bed of his truck, he drove off. I located unit 34-C and entered the room. It was very clean inside and contained nothing! There was no furniture, no bed, no heat (I discovered that Utah is cold in September!) and no hot water.

Dead tired, I threw my coat on the tile floor, and keeping my suit on, went to sleep. I awoke to a bone-chilling cold, and, here I am, back at the beginning of this book, 2,106 miles from that beloved Italian section of Allentown, Pennsylvania!

I was ready for college, but there was one problem. Looking out the window of unit 34-C, I saw nothing but prairie and the Rocky Mountains! Where the hell was Utah State University? Time to get organized. Removing the suit I had worn for over twenty-four consecutive hours, I shivered through the coldest shower I had ever taken in my life and found some clean clothing in one of my suitcases. It was then that I realized I was starving, but that would have to wait. Heading outside, I walked until I reached a road, the same road, I'm certain, that Mr. Oswald used to take me to 34-C! I began walking, hoping I was going in the right direction, when a guy in a pick-up truck pulled over and asked me if I needed a lift. At that point, I think I needed a spiritual lift more than anything! "Yes," I told him. I jumped in, he pulled away, and we were off. I asked him if he knew where the campus was, and he told me that he was headed there. Finally, something was going right. We talked as he drove, and I enjoyed his company. Heck, I enjoyed anyone's company at that moment! We arrived at an enormous campus, and it amazed me that something this big could have been this hard to find! After he dropped me off amid thousands of students hurrying in every direction, I stopped one of them and asked where I needed to go to register for class. He directed me to the fieldhouse a few blocks away, and I headed in that direction.

Entering the fieldhouse, I saw another thousand kids scurrying around from table to table. They were holding cards and carrying pens and pencils with them. I hadn't experienced any orientation, but common sense told me to make sure I had a pen with me when I left to find the school. Legend will tell you that I followed a cute blonde around the fieldhouse, selecting the same classes as she, thus ending up as an English major. It's a great story, told over and over by many of my future colleagues; however, as romantic as that may sound, it has no basis for truth!

I had an unhappy experience with high school, due in large part to my dislike for mathematics, but I always loved English class. My English professor at Moravian College had told me that I had a "strong aptitude" for English, and I should consider something in that field if I were to continue my education.

I must interject a story here- one that is important to my future. My high school homeroom teacher, chemistry teacher, and football coach by the name of Thomas Persing was second only to my dad as the man I most admired and respected, and I know how disappointed he was in me as a student when I was in his class. He told me, in so many words, that I was "wasting my life," and it always bothered me that a man whom I respected that much, thought so little of me. More on that later.

While it is true that I asked a young lady for help, and it so happened that she was very attractive, my motive, at the time, was getting registered for college. I asked her how to go about selecting courses, and she asked me what my major was. The only thing I could honestly say that interested me was English, and I told her I wanted to major in English. Naturally, she was an English major, and she suggested several courses I might like, some of them that happened to be on her registration card as well. Yes, she did help me, and I did attend some of the same classes as she, but that's where the legend ends. After signing up for eighteen credits worth of classes, it was time to make another decision. At the end of the registration, there was a sign that read, "English majors to report to room 105." Another sign read, "English teaching majors to report to room 205." I thought about Mr. Persing. I respected him for the lessons he taught me both on the football field and in the classroom. I was a terrible student, but his "life lessons" remained with me. I wanted that. I wanted to make a difference in someone's life the way he made a difference in mine! I took the stairs to the second floor and entered room 205.

After registering for classes, I walked outside and found the student center. Ravenous by this time, I ordered a sandwich and sat at a table on the patio. As I ate, I thought about another important detail. I had no idea where my apartment was, nor did I have a clue as to how to get back to it. I sat there for an hour or two wondering if I would ever see my clothing again, when I saw the guy that picked me up, driving through the campus. I almost ran several students down as I dashed into the street and flagged him down. I asked him if he could take me back to the spot where he picked me up that morning. As we drove, he told me he was looking for a room. I offered my apartment to him, letting him know he was more than welcome to become my roommate; however, I let him know that the place had no furniture. He like that idea, and we drove to 34-C. When we entered the apartment, I was shocked to find a sofa, chairs, cooking utensils and best of all, beds! Four beds, two in each bedroom! I think we might be in for more roommates! We had heat and hot water, and I was registered for classes to become an English teacher. The day had been a huge success! We found out later that the apartments were brand new and were opened for married students. However, due to the number of students in need of housing, the apartments became available to all students. We eventually gained two more roommates, one from the country of Lebanon and another from Pennsylvania!

My first class at Utah State was Freshman Composition. Students were assigned to write an essay telling about the person he or she most admired and why. The only stipulation was that we could not write about one of our parents. Since I couldn't write about my dad, the assignment was a "no-brainer" for me. I wrote my paper about Thomas Persing, my teacher and coach, whom I respected more than any man other than my father. As I already mentioned in this book, this was the man that inspired me to become a teacher. He was the reason I chose to walk up those steps to the second floor and join the rest of the students enrolling as English teaching majors. I received an A for my paper from my professor, along with a note asking me to stop by his office. As we spoke, he asked me if I had ever shared my feelings with Mr. Persing. He told me that if I hadn't, I should, as he would appreciate knowing the influence he had on my life.

33.

Gung a Din

I arrived home from my freshman year at Utah State with a fresh outlook on my old Italian neighborhood. I and two other friends from school had driven the 2,106 miles from Logan straight through, stopping only for food and gas.

In Utah, I had ridden a horse, given to me by my friend's parents who owned a horse farm in Brigham City, into the Rocky Mountains, traveled to Yellowstone, studied hard and made the Dean's List. Now, I was home, on familiar ground, seeing my friends from the neighborhood for the first time in nine months. Rollie was in Vietnam, which was cause for concern. I had lost several friends there, including the fellow who shared his Utah State brochure with me. I spent time working in the bakery with my dad, and I never lost the feel for what needed to be done, and when.

I watched the Italian men gather outside the I-Club, and I felt as if I had never left town. My dad couldn't have been prouder of what I had accomplished, but ironically, some of the older Italians and even some of my relatives considered my decision to choose college as a 'betrayal' to my dad. "How can the kid do that to his old man?" "That" referring to my leaving my dad in a lurch to become a "college boy"! Dad told me not to worry about them, and truth be told, I understood these men. They were old school Italians. Men worked for a living. My own Italian Nonna once told me, "A man's hands never get dirty by working!" I understood these men and loved every one of them.

My friends had taken different paths. Tony was now an entrepreneur, running his nightclub with Tom, and Gerry was iron-working for a living. Chas did well in his first year at Indiana University of Pennsylvania, and we enjoyed sharing stories about school.

The biggest change for me was my brother. He had grown in those few, short months, and I enjoyed spending time with him, playing fast-pitch against the Hygrade wall and hearing about his many girlfriends. I hung out, doing basically nothing for a week or two before becoming antsy. I needed to work! I was still spending my Saturdays at the bakery, but the pipeline experience left me wanting more. I got a job with an electrical contractor in charge of building a state-of-the-art basic oxygen furnace at the Bethlehem Steel. I had no idea what a basic oxygen furnace was designed to do, but I knew it had something to do with improving the production of steel. I reported to the site the following morning and met my new foreman. He took one look at me and said I was a strong-looking kid and would handle working with the wire-running crew. Again, the term "wire-running" meant no more to me than "basic oxygen," but I was ready to work.

I met with one of the guys on the crew and asked him where I should go. With his finger pointing towards the sky, he said, "Up there." I looked up and saw a group of men about eighty feet in the air, walking on beams no more than six inches wide! At that moment, I had new respect for my friend, Gerry Rizzetto, one of the iron workers putting up this building. I was afraid to ask him how I was supposed to get up there, but I didn't see any eighty-foot ladders lying around, so I bit the bullet and asked. He walked me over to one of the cranes and told me to put my foot into the hook attached to the crane's cable. He then said to me, "Grab the cable and hang on!" I did, and the next thing I knew, the cable shot straight up! Seriously, what other direction was it going to go? Shaking like a leaf, I asked the guys on the beam, "What do I do now?" One of the guys said to me, "Well, unless you intend to spend the next eight hours hanging there, step onto the beam." Where was the pipeline when I needed it?

The next thing I knew, guys were hanging loops of cable over my shoulder and handing me a bag of tools. They began walking along the beam as if it were a six-foot wide sidewalk. I, on the other hand, was moving at the speed of darkness! One of the guys turned to me and said, "Let's go, kid, or we'll be here all day!" Once again, I was "the kid," only on this job, I became known as the "college kid." Every ten feet or so, a round, steel rod extended through the beam to the floor below. I was told they were support rods and I needed to "just grab 'em and swing around to the other side." This went on for about a hundred feet. When I reached for the next support rod, instead of a steel rod, it was a welding cable dangling from the floor above. When I grabbed it and began to swing, it stretched towards me, and my entire, short life passed before my eyes! Petrified now and unable to move, I heard one of the guys say to me, "Don't worry, kid, the fall won't hurt you. It's the sudden stop that will kill you!" Construction worker humor! Gotta love it!

If the Scranton men were characters, the wire crew was a bunch of crazies! We were paid on a Thursday which I found to be an unusual payday. An armored car would arrive at the construction site, and a table would be set up. Two armed guards stood watch as the paymaster doled out cash! Thousands of dollars were on that table, and those two guards were responsible for its safety, not to mention the safety of the paymaster. While I was heading home with my pay, the wire crew was on their way to the local bar to drink and play poker. Some of those guys arrived on Friday morning without a dime to their name. It came as no surprise to me that nine of the ten guys on our crew were divorced! That said, they were good people, and I enjoyed every one of them. They were hard workers and a little too daring on that steel. They would eat lunch on the iron, eighty feet in the air, and then lie down on a six-inch girder and close their eyes! It scared the hell out of me that one of these guys would fall asleep and roll over! The fall won't hurt you. It's the sudden stop that will kill you! As the weeks wore on, I became a little more at ease on the iron, but I never took for granted where I was and never became as casual about it as they were. I remember my friend, Gerry, a life-long iron worker, telling me that those guys were hot dogs and I shouldn't emulate any of the nonsense they did on the iron.

One morning, we were running a line across the iron, and one of the guys on the crew told me we were two feet short. He told me to go to the tool shed and request the wire stretchers. I rode the crane to the ground, walked two blocks to the tool shed and asked the man in charge for the wire stretchers. He smiled at me and said, “You're working with Walter's gang, aren't you?” I told him I was, and he laughed, informing me that they pull that stunt on every new kid that joins their crew. “There's no such thing as a wire stretcher, son,” was all he said to me. I guess he could have given me the business, but that was coming soon enough! As I was walking towards the crane to return to the iron, the crew gave me a standing ovation from above. Being the “kid” isn't easy.

I spent a few days working with a pretty decent guy on the ground. We were sending conduit to the men working above, and he told me to tie off a section of pipe so they could pull it up. Several granny knots later, my fellow worker walked over and showed me the proper way to tie a section of conduit that was fast and secure. After that, I was sending the pipes to the guys on the iron at rapid speed. I thanked him for the lesson, and for not teasing me about my granny knots. He told me that everyone had to learn sometime. The next day, I was back on the iron, and it was stifling hot. We had a five-gallon cooler of water with us, and it was time for a re-fill. Being the kid, I was not surprised when Walt told me to head down and re-fill our cooler. He told me to tie it off when I got back to the site, and the guys would pull it up to the iron.

This was my golden opportunity! Remembering what I was taught, I tied a perfect electrical worker's knot on that can, and I was pumped to show off my stuff! As the guys began to hoist the can to the iron, my mind drifted to someone on the ground. I was watching a couple of guys knock down a wall with sledge hammers when, suddenly, someone screamed for me to get out of the way. I took about three steps just before the igloo cooler filled with forty pounds of water crashed to the ground! Water flew everywhere as the cooler flattened like an accordion file! Everyone in the area became quiet for about ten seconds, and then one of the guys on my crew cried out, "Oh my God, the kid tied it to the lid!" The knot was as good as any on the job, unfortunately, instead of tying it to the handle of the cooler, I had fastened it to the lid! The one thing that bothered me was the fact that the damn lid didn't come loose from the can until it was seventy feet in the air! This was the ultimate humiliation! I had no choice but to return to the iron and take it like a man! Meanwhile, one of the other guys went to the tool shed, picked up a new cooler, and hoisted it to the top of the iron.

I was hoping I could get back to the tool shed at the end of the day, drop off my tools and quietly disappear; however, as I walked towards the shed, I saw one of the guys from our crew standing on top of the trailer with about two hundred electricians, iron workers and laborers gathered around him. I arrived just in time to hear him say, "and then he tied it to the lid!" The place went crazy! I thought about turning around and heading to my car, but turning in my tools at the end of the day was mandatory. I could always drop my tool belt, turn around, and walk to my car. Maybe the pipeline was looking for workers! Instead, I strolled to the shed as cool as I could, high-fiving workers along the way. For the rest of my time on that job, whenever I passed by anyone, I was greeted with my new nick-name. "Hey, Gung a Din, how ya doin?"

I wasn't very savvy when it came to union business, but I became educated about it very quickly. It seems that a small portion of wall needed to be removed before the iron workers could set a steel post in place. One of the iron workers picked up a sledge hammer and was ready to knock the wall down when a member of the laborer's union told him that was work for a laborer. The iron-worker said he could take the wall down in two minutes, but the union leader for the laborers said "no." It happened to be a Saturday, and the laborers weren't working that day. A "disagreement" between the iron workers and the union leader for the laborers became a bit heated, and all work ceased. All this happened before I had arrived for work that morning. The laborers were notified, and a group of them showed up with picket signs. No work was going to be done that day until a laborer knocked down that wall. Oblivious to all of this, I parked my car and began strolling across the railroad tracks on my way to pick up my badge at the electrical workers' shack. Suddenly, a laborer picked up a two-by-four and aimed it at my head, telling me that if I took one more step, he would "knock my head off."

I liked the work, and the money was great, but I was a fast-learner. This man did not want me to cross those railroad tracks, and I was more than happy to oblige! Turning around, I headed back to my car and drove home for a relaxing day of peace and quiet. I learned, the next, day, that a laborer was brought in to take down the wall. He swung the sledge hammer once, and the wall tumbled to the ground! Union rules dictated that the man receive a half-day's salary for his work, and because it was Saturday, he was to receive time and a half! I really needed to get back to school!

The wire crew was finally given a job on the ground. We had to feed wire through the entire plant before it could be connected to the main power transformer. Feeding a wire through a building can't be that difficult. Most of us have fed a wire through a wall to a receptacle in our house at one time or another. However, this wire was three inches in diameter and weighed well over a thousand pounds! The wire was delivered on a wooden spool by truck and hoisted from the truck bed with one of the enormous cranes on site. The spool was at least fifteen feet high, and the wire had to be fed through a steel track welded near the ceiling in the bowels of the plant. This would be done by feeding a steel cable along the track until it reached the exterior of the building where the spool of wire would be attached to the end of the cable. With men on the other end, near the transformer operating a winch, the cable would slowly pull the large wire along the track until it reached the other end. Our crew was responsible for "feeding" the huge wire into the building by turning the spool and soaping the wire as it entered to make it move more easily through the channel. Before all of this could take place, someone had to crawl through the metal track, which was less than a foot from the ceiling, and scrape any burrs from the track that might cause the wire to hang up. "Someone" meant me!

"The kid will do it."

"Yeah, let Gung a Din crawl in there."

And so, I did. Fortunately, I didn't have the beer gut that many on the wire crew had, but it wouldn't have made any difference. I was going to be selected no matter what kind of belly I had! While the men on the wire crew occupied themselves with another task, I spent an entire eight-hour day crawling along the track, scraping burrs clear. It was August, and it was hot! Next door, men were pouring molten, white-hot steel into huge kettles, and that pushed the temperature even higher! I finished the task while losing a few pounds, and we were ready to run the wire. As the wire snaked into the building and crawled slowly through the track, we fed the spool into the wall at the rate of about one foot every ten minutes! As we got to the end of the spool and fed the final foot of wire into the hole, one of the guys received a message on his walkie-talkie. "Only two more feet to go" cried the man on the other end. We looked at each other in total bewilderment. We didn't have another two feet of wire! If ever a "wire stretcher" did exist, this was the time! We spent the next day retracting the wire and rolling it back onto the spool. There was no such thing as splicing this baby! A new wire had to be delivered. Eventually, the new wire was fed through the track, and attached to the transformer, and I was grateful I wasn't going to have to re-scrape the channel a second time!

On any large industrial project, dozens of portable toilets are scattered about the building site. Such was the case with the project on which we worked at the Bethlehem Steel. Whenever a worker entered one of these "porta-johns" he was subjected to mischief from the men on the iron. I remember one man entering the bathroom on a hot, August afternoon to take care of business. One of the guys rode the crane to the ground, wrapped a steel cable around the "porta-potty," hooked it to the crane and scampered back up the iron. The crane operator hoisted the potty, with the "man on the throne" about fifteen feet in the air and locked down the crane. As I said, it was a hot day, and this guy was in no mood for bathroom humor. The trapped worker screamed expletives beyond words commonly heard around a construction site! When the operator finally set it down fifteen minutes later, and the red-faced man charged out the door, everyone on the ground began to scatter. Those of us on the iron, eighty feet in the air, were safe. I was never so glad to be a part of the "high iron" crew as I was that day!

Before I left that job at the end of the summer, I had one unique and pleasant experience. During World War II, before Dad joined the Navy, he was working at the Bethlehem Steel in the gun shop.

The shop contained enormous lathes which were used to turn down and cut barrels for our country's battleships. We had a lathe at home in my father's workshop, but these lathes were huge! Weighing tons, they were almost thirty feet long, and were in constant motion getting the gun barrels ready for our ships to fight the war. The last two weeks of my time, I was sent to the gun shop to assist an electrician who was part of the renovation crew, changing the now defunct gun shop into a new facility. The lathes that my dad had worked were still there, and it gave me chills to think of the room, so many years earlier, and the men, including my dad who worked there as part of the war effort. When I told him where I had been working for the past two weeks, he became excited and asked me all about the lathes and the new plans for the shop. It was a cool moment, and the perfect time to say goodbye to cranes, girders, and crazy guys! It was time to head back to school!

34.

An Emmy for Ben

After graduating from college in 1969, I was hired by the Southern Lehigh School District to teach English in the junior high school. The school would be re-structured to become a middle school the following year.

Attempting to recall highlights from a 36-year career in the classroom would be an exercise in futility – too many stories to tell, but a few things stand out in my memory.

My first principal was a fair, but tough man. Stan was an old-school Pennsylvania Dutchman, and he and I seemed to get off on the wrong foot. I recall walking into the faculty room during the first week of my tenure and removing my suit coat. I proceeded to hang the coat on one of the window latches in the room. Without saying a word, my new boss walked over to the window, removed my suit coat from the window latch, and dropped it on the floor. I stood there in amazement, not able to speak, and was told by the gruff, old Dutchman, "The window is not a coat hanger, Durich."

OK, strike one with this guy, but I wasn't going to allow him to get to me. Two days later, I went in the faculty room for a cup of coffee, only to discover that my coffee cup, fashioned with love on a potter's wheel by my wife, was nowhere in sight. I asked one of the other teachers if he had seen my cup and was told that Stan had removed it from the table and taken it with him when he left the room. I soon found a note in my mailbox telling me to see Stan about my cup, so I knocked on his office door and went inside.

Deciding not to make this easy, he continued his work until I asked him what he needed to see me about. He reached into his desk drawer and retrieved my coffee cup. "Durich, do you know what a cupboard is for?" he asked. The answer was obvious, and I replied, "It's used to store our cups." Without another word, he handed me my cup and went back to his work.

Strike two! This was going to be a long (or very short) career! Things settled down after that, and I was cruising through my first year of teaching without any more visits from the boss. My English classes were working on reports in the school library, when one of my students approached me. She was working on a report about suicide and asked me if there were any additional sources besides the library to find information. I suggested that she might be able to speak to someone from the Suicide Prevention Center who might be able to help her. I advised her to have her questions written down before calling, and I told her I wanted to read the questions before she called. I also told her to identify herself and let the person know her purpose for calling and made sure she let me know if they needed to speak with me. I became involved with other students, and the young lady in question decided to go "off script." She called the suicide hotline, and her first words to the person on the phone were, "What should I do if someone is threatening to jump off the roof of our school?" The responder asked for her location, and ten minutes later, a fire engine, an emergency vehicle, and a police car came careening into the parking lot of our school. Almost as fast, Stan came speeding into the library, bellowing, "Durich, what's going on?" The reader is probably thinking, "Strike three" but I survived that debacle and made it through my first year of teaching without ruffling Stan's feathers again.

My coffee cup came into play again during the beginning of my second year. I walked into the faculty room to find that my cup had been used by someone as an ashtray. There was no one in the room with whom to vent my frustration, so I left a note on the table, letting everyone know that it was my coffee cup, and the person who chose to use it as an ash tray was extremely inconsiderate. When I returned to the faculty room at the end of the day, I found my coffee cup filled to the brim with cigarette butts, ashes, and a banana peel. I didn't say a word, but my plan for revenge had been born.

I remained in my classroom until almost five p.m., before making my way to the faculty room, which was deserted by then. Using a large cardboard box I found on the loading dock, I removed every cup from the cupboard and placed them into the box. Using a ladder I found on the loading dock, I removed one of the tiles from the ceiling in the hallway outside the faculty room, put the box of cups in the ceiling, and replaced the ceiling tile. The following morning, I strolled into the faculty room with my cup, which I had stored in my desk before leaving school. I walked over to the coffee urn and filled my cup amidst a room of hostile stares! I was the only one in the room with a cup of coffee, and I looked around and asked, "Isn't anyone having coffee this morning?" I expected a call from Stan, since his was one of the cups I stored in the box, but it never came.

Most everyone showed up the following day with a new cup from home, and I waited a few weeks before retrieving the box from the ceiling and putting the cups back in the cupboard. No one ever mentioned it again. I want to add that I loved these people and enjoyed every one of them for years to come. Stan and I became good friends, and he even asked me to take on the additional position of yearbook advisor. Stan was instrumental in the design of our middle school. When it came time for his retirement, I assigned a few students from my yearbook staff to interview him and add a special section to the yearbook with photos showing his work on the building. I presented the book, embossed with his name, at his retirement dinner.

In 1990, our principal asked the faculty if anyone would be interested in starting a television studio in the middle school. The studio would be used to broadcast morning announcements, lunch schedules and the events of the day at the middle school. I told her that I was interested and would be willing to give it a try. Recruiting a group of students, I was given a small storage room in the rear of the school library to get started. The studio and staff of students would become my homeroom. We met each morning to begin planning this new venture.

One of the guys on my staff, a student by the name of Ben Weinberger, knew more about TV equipment than all of us put together. We were given a small budget with which to get started. Our first equipment came in the form of two very old security cameras that had been used on school buses to monitor the students. The cameras weren't even equipped with tripods, so we built our own. The high school donated some of their old studio equipment, and Ben worked his magic. He made all the connections, and we were ready to broadcast to the classrooms. Lisa, our principal, worked out a deal with a, now-defunct, company that offered televisions for classrooms provided we ran their morning show. Once the TVs were installed in the classrooms, we were ready for our first broadcast. As two of our girls sat behind a table with their announcements printed on sheets of paper, we began our first broadcast with the pledge of allegiance and a moment of silence. The program lasted about five minutes and went off without a hitch.

Ben was a wheeler-dealer, and having money left in our budget, he asked me if we could go to an electronics store to upgrade our equipment. Lisa gave us the go-ahead, and I drove Ben to the store to do some shopping. Ben was amazing! Not intimidated in the least by the people running the store, Ben threw technical terms at those guys that neither they nor I understood. When it came to pay for the equipment with our paltry budget, Ben convinced them that we would be doing them a service by providing free advertising, and we walked out of there with every piece of equipment we needed at a very incredible cost!

In no time, our studio had gone high-tech, and our productions rivaled those of our high school. I said to Ben, "Someday, I am going to read about your winning an Emmy!" A few years ago, Ben sent me a message on Facebook, complete with a photograph of him and his staff holding an Emmy presented by The National Academy of Television Arts and Sciences for outstanding achievement in technical or engineering development.

About three years ago, I received another message from a former student by the name of Adrian Kulp. He had written a book entitled Dad Or Alive, the story of his experiences as a stay-at-home dad. I attended his book signing and had him sign several copies, which I shared with my family. Since then, Adrian has moved to Nashville to take a job on radio and has written another book.

During the last few years of my teaching career, I had my eighth-grade classes write a research paper on a career which interested them. Using career files from our library as well as available library computers, they found a plethora of information, and the reports were both informative and interesting. I began to think about taking this idea to another level. The following year, I had them write a resume as if they were going to apply for a job in that field. I made it clear that lying on a resume was inappropriate; however, for this assignment, they could include whatever information they felt was necessary to get the job. We discussed the proper way to dress for an interview and what type of questions they expected from the interviewer.

The career unit continued to grow, and the following year, I added a job fair. Contacting dozens of local business people, merchants, and service people, many of whom were parent volunteers, we set up stations in the gym for each presenter, and had the students sign up for four visitations. Our student council provided breakfast for the presenters along with a small gift, and the first job fair began. Using parent volunteers to act as interviewers, I assigned each student an interview time and location. During the job fair, it was the responsibility of the student to leave the gym on time for his or her interview. The student presented his or her resume to the interviewer, and questions began. The interviewers were given a rating sheet which they completed at the end of the interview, and I collected them at the end of the day.

The first job fair was a rousing success, and the unit became an institution at the middle school for years after I left. I was asked to present the unit at an educator's conference, and received many requests from teachers throughout the valley for additional information about the program.

I spent thirty-six years teaching eighth-grade English and coaching high school football and track. By the time I retired in 2004, I had taught and coached over five thousand young men and women, many with whom I keep in touch on Facebook today. It warms my heart to hear stories about their careers, children, and, yes, even grandchildren!

During my first year in the classroom at Southern Lehigh, our principal was taking the superintendent from another school district on a tour of our building. The principal brought the gentleman into my classroom while I was teaching my English class, and, very quietly, they observed my students and me as I continued my lesson. I looked at the two men standing in the back of the room and realized that the superintendent was Thomas Persing! He looked at me, smiled, and winked. I thought about my English Composition professor from Utah State, telling me that I needed to share my feelings about my former coach and teacher with him, but I never did. That wink said everything I needed to know. His disappointment in me was gone. After they left, and my class was dismissed, I sat at my desk and cried.

35.

Friends and Family

I married the girl whom I kissed goodbye at the airport on that cold, drizzly day I left for Utah, and Jane and I remained together for almost thirty years. Our two lovely daughters, Amy and Jennifer, have blessed us with four beautiful grandchildren. When I watch my daughters with their children, I am awestruck and grateful for the example set by their mother. Jane is an extremely gifted artist as well. My sister, Anita, worked as a laboratory technician at Georgetown Hospital in Myrtle Beach for over twenty years before retiring and returning to Pennsylvania to be near her three boys.

My dear friend, Tony, became a decorated undercover detective in Philadelphia and received recognition in the Philadelphia Inquirer for his work in law-enforcement. Chas graduated from Indiana University of Pennsylvania. Ironically, the man who asked me in the diner so many years ago, "Do we really want to walk on steel girders for the rest of our lives?" joined our dear friend, Gerry Rizetto, as an iron worker! It didn't really surprise me. Chas is a hard-worker, and iron work just seemed to suit him. Both Gerry and Chas have since retired, and Chas spends his time fishing and concentrating on his art. He is an amazing artist!

Rollie survived his time in Vietnam and shared stories about having been spit upon in airports when he returned to the states. I know he lost friends there, and it breaks my heart to see young men, asked to put their lives on the line for their country, subjected to such disrespect! Rollie authored a beautiful book entitled The

Little Boy In The Tree, honoring his son, Andrew, who lost his life in Iraq. He and his wife now live in Ellicott City, Maryland, not very far from our home in Lewes. He and I keep in touch on Facebook, and, recently, he sent me a photo of the little flag I mailed to him when he was in Vietnam!

Sadly, one of the members of our group, Ritchie Petrafesa, passed away recently. Two years ago, I traveled with Tony's brother, Louie, to a hunting camp in central Pennsylvania to help with some work that needed to be done at the camp before winter. Ritchie was at the camp, and it was the first time I had seen him in over twenty years! He and I sat in the kitchen and talked for hours, sharing stories from our past. It was the last time I saw him, and I was so grateful for having had those few, short hours with him in the kitchen that day.

My cousin, Ron, another member of the "group" – the guy who released the brake on the truck, the guy who drove our truck to the pig hunt, and the guy who drove his Packard over the pipes behind Haney's Pig Stand, now lives in San Jose, California, where he spent the last thirty years working as an estimator for an electrical contractor.

The Gentrys would have the same problem as the Beatles as far as re-uniting for a concert! Eddie, our smooth-voiced crooner, passed away a few years ago, as did Tom, our band-leader, who was short on talent, but long on heart! Skip, our soft-spoken lead guitar player, runs a hobby shop somewhere in North Carolina. Chuck, our sax player, now lives in Pittsburgh with his family where he emcees a local sports radio show called *The Maestro*.

Whenever Nori and I travel to Pennsylvania to visit my family, we make it a point to get together with as many of our group as possible. Occasionally, we will meet Tony's brother, Louie, and his wife, as well as Rosie and her husband for dinner. Our favorite gathering place used to be Louie's Italian Restaurant. I grew up with Louie Belletieri, and I used to deliver our bread to Gino's Steak Shop, Louie's father's place. After delivering the steak rolls, I'd sit down at the counter, and Louie or his dad would serve me one of their delicious steak sandwiches! Louie eventually opened his own restaurant, and there was no better Italian food in the city of Allentown! Louie retired this past year, and it broke the hearts of everyone who spent evenings there enjoying fine food, laughter, and always a table visit from Louie, who would spend time sitting with every customer in his restaurant!

Toward the end of my teaching career, I was living in a small farmhouse in Fogelsville, Pennsylvania. After a few less than interesting dates with people I had met through an online dating site, I lost interest. I had discovered that loneliness was all it is cracked up to be, and just enjoyed an occasional evening out with friends. And then it happened!

With my friend Louie at his restaurant. Best Italian food in the valley!

36.

Finding Nori

While doing some work on my computer at home in preparation for a classroom lesson, I noticed a message that had popped up on my screen. Someone from the Annapolis area of Maryland had seen my profile on the dating site and was interested in chatting with me. I instantly enjoyed her sense of humor and found her to be extremely charming. We began sharing stories about our lives, and I was fascinated by her career in theater.

We continued to exchange messages online for a month, and I found myself looking forward to her messages and disappointed when they were not there. Through email, we grew more and more connected. We talked about my driving to Maryland to visit her. She was in the middle of rehearsals for her starring role in Mame at that time, and her traveling to Pennsylvania would have been difficult. My sense of direction has been well documented earlier in this book, and coward that I was, I told her that it "probably wasn't a good idea to pursue this relationship further." With my limitations, I just couldn't see a future in beginning a relationship with someone one hundred and eighty miles away! She told me that she fully intended to meet me, and if she had to, she and her dog, Bimini, were going to jump in the car, motor to Fogelsville and drive down Main Street, beeping her horn until I came out of my house!

I didn't take her seriously until she told me she made accommodations at the Glasbern Inn in Fogelsville and was driving to Pennsylvania to have dinner with me. The date was June 1, 2004 – a date I will always remember! I arrived at my farmhouse after school and decided to go for a run before getting ready for my dinner date. I checked my answering machine and heard her voice for the first time. She told me she was in room thirty-two at the Glasbern Inn, and I should meet her there before we went to dinner in the inn's dining room. I changed into my workout gear and went to the park for a run. About a mile into my run, a storm passed through, and a bolt of lightning struck a tree branch about fifty yards in front of me. With a loud crack, the branch dropped to the ground, and I wondered if it were a sign of things to come. On the way back to my house, I stopped and bought a single rose.

I arrived at the Inn and knocked on the door of room 32. When the door opened, a very beautiful lady reached out and hugged me. I had been holding the rose in front of me, and as she hugged me, I could feel thorns sticking through my shirt into my chest! OK - lightning, thorns in my chest. Seriously? What was I getting myself into? Her name was Nori, and she and I enjoyed a delightful dinner filled with conversation and laughter.

A few weeks later, it was time for me to make the journey to Maryland, a minor detail for most people, but for me, a perilous adventure! My plan was to drive south and see Nori's performance as Mame. At that time, I had an antique flip phone with no apps, no GPS, and no car phone charger. With meticulous preparation, I left Fogelsville early to allow for all contingencies, knowing the dreaded trip was going to be anything but smooth sailing. I still couldn't know how "un-smooth" it was going to end up! About an hour later, as I was happily driving past Philadelphia, I began thinking about which outfit I should wear to the theater that night. Like another lightning bolt, it suddenly occurred to me that I had left my suitcase in Fogelsville! I debated continuing the trip to Maryland and buying all new clothing when I arrived, but I sadly resigned myself to making a U-turn all the way back to Fogelsville instead.

Upon arriving at my home, I called Nori, who asked me how

close I was to her home. When I told her I was in Fogelsville, there was dead silence on her end. I wondered if she had second thoughts at that point, but there was no turning back now.

My sweet Nori and me.

I made it to Maryland, which amazed me, but then managed to miss an exit and ended up in a parking lot at Baltimore Washington International Airport. My phone had about eight percent left in its charge, and my gas gauge was barely above empty as I pulled into the lot at BWI and turned off the ignition. Praying my cell phone didn't conk out, I called Nori, and once again, she asked me where I was. More silence followed as I revealed I was at BWI Airport. At this point, I was thinking that she probably wondered if she would see me at all before the curtain rose on stage that evening.

"Stay right there, don't move!" Those were her words. Did this girl realize I couldn't move if I wanted to? I had no idea to where I would be moving. A short while later, my phone rang. It was Nori, telling me to look across the runway to my right. I saw Nori standing by her car, waving. She drove to where I was parked, and I sheepishly followed her to her house. Was this long-distance relationship ever going to work?

That night, I was awestruck by Nori's performance on stage, and when the show ended, I was the first one on my feet to give her a standing ovation! At the cast party that evening, other cast members teased me. They said they never saw anyone jump up for a standing ovation that fast before!

Sixteen years later, Nori and I are still together, living in Lewes, Delaware, just a short, three -hour drive from my old Italian neighborhood in Allentown, Pennsylvania.

37.

Reflections

A few years ago, Nori and I drove over to the old Italian neighborhood. We had been living on the southside of Allentown at the time and wanted to visit the place where I grew up. As we drove through the streets, I remembered the street cleaner truck that sprayed our feet and splashed dirt from the street on our clothes. The hucksters, with their trucks filled with produce were gone, but I could still recall their voices as they shouted "Huckster!" Gone, too, were the pony man and the umbrella man, carrying their cameras and grinding wheels along the sidewalks.

The row houses with their freshly washed porch steps and banisters, coated with a fresh layer of brilliant white paint, were now dingy and gray. Colorful awnings, once draped across the porch fronts were gone, and porches that once held furniture were now filled with trash cans and auto parts. It really didn't matter that the furniture was gone. No one sat outside sharing stories with neighbors while reading the morning paper.

The back yards, once filled with rose bushes and hydrangeas bordering manicured lawns were filled with gravel and stone and had become lots for rusted automobiles parked within their boundaries. The victory gardens had been paved over and were filled with abandoned automobiles. Weathered boards covered the windows of the Bonney Forge and the Hygrade Silk Mill, and the lot where so many fun-filled baseball games had been played was an over-grown field filled with trash!

The older Italian men and women have since passed, and the younger people who called this neighborhood their home have, one at a time, married and moved away to homes in the suburbs. The people who settled there from the old world remained there for their entire lives. The Italian section of Allentown was their home- for life!

As we traveled through the streets, I envisioned people sitting on their porches talking and laughing as they shared stories of their day. I heard laughter coming from the children playing games of hop-scotch on the sidewalk. I could still see Dad's movie projector shining light on the screen at the end of the yard as neighbors munched on popcorn and drank Kool-aid and watched cartoons! Across the street, the sound of a ball meeting somebody's bat with a loud crack could be heard, and the thump of a basketball on the street meant a game was taking place.

I didn't see a dark, empty Italian Club building across from Russoli's market. I recalled people, dressed in their "Sunday Best," laughing as they walked up the steps to the front door of their beloved I-Club ready for an evening of pasta, chicken, wine and dancing. I heard the music as the band played Italian songs while everyone enjoyed dinner followed by a glass of Weee-O!

Russoli's window was brightly polished with a display of penny candy awaiting kids with their pockets filled with coins in search of their favorite confection. Between the club and Russoli's market, the street was filled with neighbors readying their instruments and waiting for Mr. Frasetto to lead them in a Father's Day concert while the balloon man tied balloons to the wrists of excited children.

Coming from the little alley by the name of Carrot Street, I could once again smell the sweet aroma of warm bread on the cooling rack as my Zio Top sang along to the music from the radio. I saw Gigi DeMarki walking into the bakery with his dime, prepared to fill his sack with bread, and Dewey Trenge carrying his hand-made neck-ties into the shop before departing with one loaf of star bread. Men gathered in front of our luncheonette, eating ice cream cones or hot dogs as they talked about the Yankees or the next I-Club baseball game. Christmas music echoed from my sister's reel to reel tape recorder, as the group baked and decorated cookies in Dad's bakery.

I could still see Big John's limo pulling into the alley, his men opening the door for him as he entered the bakery for his bread. I remember the flour settling on his long, black coat. Nor could I ever forget John telling the man at the clothing factory, "The kid's gonna pick out some suits."

The taste of warm butter on a roll fresh from our oven or a chunk of salami from a neighbor, still makes my mouth water. I think of the times Dad used to finish his lunch and retire to our basement, put a Mario Lanza record on his record player and take a nap. I used to walk up to the back of his lounge chair and smell his hair. It always smelled of flour, and I loved it.

I still remember watching Tony as we waded into the pond at Castle Rock to rescue the damsels trapped in eighteen inches of water and Rollie's Simca making cracking sounds as it turned a corner with us rolling around in the rear seat.

It's easy to see my mom, strong and athletic, firing a bowling ball down the alley on a school night at the Italian Club as Sis, my dad and I looked on while consuming steak sandwiches. I still remember the Redi-whip cans exploding and launching themselves into the sky, and the exhilaration of swinging from a rope into an open box car.

The raucous sounds coming from the pinball machines at Doc's still ring in my ears as we sat, pouring over comic books and magazines we never intended to buy! The longest conversation I have ever experienced returns to my mind as I smile, remembering my scripted phone call to my first girlfriend, and my mentor, Rollie telling me to allow her to take two steps up the stairs and stop to "equalize" our height!

Groups of people, young and old, dressed in their suits and sport-coats, walked through the streets making their rounds on Christmas morning. As they passed one another on the sidewalk, they wished each other a Merry Christmas before moving on to the next house for some brandy and their favorite baked goods. Memories of Christmas in our Italian neighborhood are some of the most vivid of all. It was a special time, made more special by the people who lived there. Dad's elaborate light displays were amazing, as were the beautiful paintings done by Rosie every year. None of us will ever forget that midnight mass, watching the doors of our church open and the people trying to get past the gentleman and his car wedged between the sidewalk and the door. Instead of becoming angry, he wished us a Merry Christmas 'ere he drove out of sight,'

As Nori and I drove down Cedar Street, I looked to my right at the darkened parking lot behind our beloved Italian Club. As I looked at more abandoned vehicles littering the lot, my mind took me back to a time when the lot was clay, rather than asphalt, and bright lights illuminated the evening sky. The sound of a carousel could be heard throughout the neighborhood, while music played, and people ate French fries and cotton candy. A Ferris wheel turned in the night toward the stars, as the annual summer carnival brought our Italian neighborhood to life!

Memories of "Eee-oh Eleven" as the "boys of summer" rode the bakery truck to Chun's pig farm to capture "lunch" for our picnic with the girls, come flooding back to me. I remember "Shrimp Boats," BB-guns, pea-shooters, rubber snakes, bingo stands, wire stretchers, globs of grease, hood ornaments, Beatle wigs, accordions, demo records, Gunga Din, the Moose, butch wax, empty prune juice bottles, Tommy Check, and Mr. Oswald. All these things and people made up the fabric of my life.

This was the Italian section of Allentown, an area settled in the 1900's in Allentown's first, sixth, ninth, and tenth wards encompassing an area west of the Lehigh River to Seventh Street, south to the Little Lehigh Creek and north to the Whitehall line. This was our neighborhood. The sights and sounds I just mentioned are the ones imbedded in my heart. Our group has moved on to new places and new adventures in our lives. That may be true, but as my dad once said to me, "It's not the destination, but the journey," and what a journey it has been!